You are not accidental. The world needs you.

Without you, something will be missing in existence, and nobody can replace it.

Osho, Indian philosopher

Dedication

*To my husband, Dom, and sons,
Francesco and Alessandro.*

Thank you for being you and for helping me discover the 'Courage to Be' me.

Courage To Be
By Carlii Lyon
Published by Infinite Identity Press
First published in the United Kingdom in 2025

ISBNs:
Paperback: 978-1-7642188-0-1
eBook: 978-1-7642188-1-8

Copyright © 2025 Carlii Lyon

Creative and Design Spiffing Publishing www.spiffingpublishing.com

All rights reserved. No part of this book may be reproduced, stored in a retrieval system, or transmitted in any form or by any means, electronic, mechanical, photocopying, recording, or otherwise, without the prior written permission of the publisher, except in the case of brief quotations embodied in critical articles or reviews.

The moral right of the author has been asserted.

This book is a work of non-fiction. While every effort has been made to ensure accuracy, the publisher and author accept no responsibility for errors or omissions, or for any loss or damage caused by reliance on the information contained within.

Any references to brands, organisations, or individuals are made in good faith and do not imply endorsement or affiliation. All trademarks and registered trademarks remain the property of their respective owners.

COURAGE to BE

Small steps for a *BIG* life

Carlii Lyon

INFINITE IDENTITY PRESS

Contents

Introduction p11

MIND

The Life-Changing Magic of 'I' p20
Make Space for Grace p27
Embrace What You DK p32
Speak Back to the Little You p35
Quieten Your Inner Drama Queen (or King) p39
Stop Learning, Start Doing p44
Channel the Power of Your Attention p48
Turn Memories into Mojo p52
Trust Your Intuition Always p56
Talk To Your Future Self Regularly p60
Think About Your Funeral Everyday p66

BODY

Make Mindset Part of Your Beauty Routine p78
Always Wear Red Lipstick (Metaphorically Speaking) ... p82
Be the First to Smile p85
Choose Commitments Over Your Feelings p88
Learn to Recognise the Signs of Growth p92
Tap into the Charismatic Power of Caring p95
Unlock Confidence by Changing Your Pose p99
Embody the Magic of Serendipity p102
Act Your Spirit, Not Your Age p107
Reinvent Yourself from the Outside In p111

BRAND

Create a Personal Brand with Purpose p118
Beware of The Thoughts p136
Practise Intentional Authenticity p140
Avoid Becoming a Stereotype p146
Creatively Package Your Ideas p151
Put a Higher Value on Things You Find Easy p154
Become Selectively Famous p157
Lead Thought in the Way Only You Can p162
Be Consistent with What You Share Online p165
Learn to Network from the Stage p169
Master the Art of Asking for What You Want p175
Invite a New Network into Your Life p181
Celebrate Rejection and Criticism p187
Never Put a Deadline on Becoming the Best Version of Yourself p192
Conclusion p194
Acknowledgements p198
Recommended Reading p201
Let's Stay in Touch p202
About the Author p204

Introduction

To be, or not to be, that is the question.

William Shakespeare, *Hamlet*

In 2019, I published an article on LinkedIn that went viral. The article was viewed well over a million times. I received messages from around the world. I was even invited to join several religions (true story!). The article's title was *Beware of These Three Thoughts on the Path to Putting Yourself Out There*.

I am not surprised the article went viral. It had nothing to do with me and everything to do with the fact that so many people struggle to find the *courage to be* who they want to be and put themselves out there.

What is important for you to understand is that, up until that point, I was a world-leading expert at **not** putting myself out there. Fear, the weight of the imposter syndrome on my shoulders, and an overall sense of insecurity always held me back. I did not have the *courage to be* seen, heard and known. The irony was that my career, up until that point, centred around shaping, managing and elevating the personal brands of high-profile individuals. I was exceptional at putting others out there, but as a high school dropout I was riddled with self-doubt. I struggled to apply to myself the thinking and methodologies I promoted to others. This disconnect wasn't a problem ... until it was.

On extended maternity leave, I was confronted with the harsh reality that I had become invisible. When I was acting in the role of personal publicist for my high-profile clients, lots of people wanted to know me and be connected. The minute I stepped out of the role, I realised I lost all visibility and any form of influence. Suddenly, I had no personal profile. I had been so adamant that I belonged 'behind the scenes' that I felt I had permanently secured my place there.

Like many people I meet today, I made the mistake of thinking my work was my source of worth. I bought into the lie that my role was the only thing that gave me credibility and value. Without it, I lost all sense of identity. I was at sea, feeling small, and unsure of what the future would hold. I reminisced of a past filled with big ideas, dreams and ambitions. It all felt like such a distant memory.

> *I was lost, feeling small, and unsure*
> *of what the future would hold.*

Everything changed after my husband Dom was brave enough to call me out on playing small. I will never forget the moment it came up. We were sitting on the lounge, the kids were in bed, and we were watching television (a rare occurrence for me). He leaned over, gently touched my knee and said, "*Honey, you haven't washed your hair in a week. You've been wearing the same clothes every day, and I can tell you are not yourself.*" He was right; the only problem was that I didn't know who 'myself' was anymore.

I knew I wanted my life to mean something. I was here, living this life for a purpose and meant for greater things. I felt haunted by the words of nearly all my high school teachers who said I had potential: I *knew* I wasn't living up to my full potential. Having babies was easily the best thing I had (and still have) ever done, but I wanted more. What stood between me and the life I knew I wanted to live was the *courage to be* who I wanted to be – out loud.

This ache reminds me of my favourite children's book by Kobi Yamada titled *Maybe – A Story About the Endless Potential in All of Us*. The book's opening line is:

> *Have you ever wondered why you are here? You are the only you there ever has been or ever will be. You have so much to offer.*

Kobi Yamada's words spoke to me. I knew I had more to offer and, you know, you have more to offer.

It took my husband to call me out on my self-sabotaging behaviour, and for me to realise things would only change if I dared to change. The following day, bolstered by the conversation the night before and determined to take constructive steps towards the future, I started googling. I don't know what I was looking for, but I came across a YouTube clip published by Gary Vaynerchuck, the matter-of-fact truth-sayer and entrepreneurial superstar. In the video, he said, "Get the f#ck on with it and stop whingeing." I decided to do just that.

I opened Facebook and mustered up the courage to post in a businesswomen's networking group. I introduced myself, explained my experience, and ended by saying I would love to find a way to support women in business.

The response was overwhelming. I was inundated with women asking for support with their personal branding. I quickly put a Word document together explaining how I could help and created a $300 Squarespace website within a week. This was the beginning of one of the most exciting chapters in my career – a chapter I am still living and, hopefully, one that shapes the rest of my days.

Fast-forward to today: I have the privilege of travelling worldwide (literally and virtually) to speak about personal branding and the power of putting yourself out there. I have worked with teams from iconic brands such as The Financial Times, L'Oreal, Microsoft, Volvo, Warner Discovery Group and Spotify, to name a few. As a personal branding coach, I have had the opportunity to support some of the smartest people I have ever met, and my work has been featured in top-tier media outlets.

I am so grateful to my past self for having the courage to take that first step to be seen, even when she didn't know what the outcome would be. As they say: You don't have to see the whole staircase; just take the first step. I sincerely hope that reading this book inspires your first step.

This hope takes me back to why I wrote the LinkedIn article mentioned above. The one thing I know for sure is this: if people can't see you, they don't know who you are and what you do, how can they decide whether they want to work, partner, collaborate, invest, follow, befriend and even date you? When we have the *courage to be* who we want to be and allow ourselves to be seen, heard and known, we can attract the right people, places and opportunities into our lives that lead us to the big life we know we are capable of living.

> *You don't have to see the whole staircase; just take the first step.*

The word 'courage' comes from the Old French word *corage*, which in turn comes from the French word *coeur*, meaning heart. Once upon a time, to have courage meant to speak from one's heart. I love that idea. *Courage to Be* is about speaking, living and loving from one's heart.

My guess is that you want to live a big life, and you know deep down you can do that. You also know the only way that is possible is if you to have the *courage to be* who you want to be and put yourself out there. On this journey, you are going to discover practical ways to help you do that on the level of mind, body and brand. These ideas and strategies have been game-changing for me and my clients; hopefully, there is something here that will work for you too.

Courage to Be is designed to be read in the way that serves you best. That might be by reading all the chapters in order or by picking and choosing what you need at any one time. Each chapter can stand alone and, at the same time, perfectly complements all the other ideas presented here.

The 3 core beliefs imbued into every word of *Courage to Be* are:

1. You are a soul-centred spiritual being having a human experience. From the soul level, you are connected to an infinite source of power, wisdom and intelligence.

2. Fear, insecurity and self-doubt will forever be part of the human experience. The goal is not to banish these feelings but to accept them for what they are and rise to meet your soul's purpose, regardless of your human limitations.

3. We can only accomplish great things when we tap into the power of the collective. Success is never achieved alone. By bravely putting ourselves out there, we can attract the people, places and opportunities that will help us fulfil our soul's purpose and lift others along the way.

It's no coincidence that you are reading this book right now. I hope this is not just a book you read then leave on the shelf. I have many books like that. My wish is that this book is an experience and one that inspires real action – that it becomes the signpost and roadmap you were looking for and which leads you to find the *courage to be* everything you want.

I hope by the time you've finished with this, your book is worn out, underlined and scribbled in, with ear-tagged pages. I want it to be the friend that supports you, the cheerleader that motivates you, and the mentor that holds your hand every step of the way. I also have books like this. They are among my most treasured possessions.

Finally, even if we never meet in person, I thank you for allowing me into your life, mind and journey. It is a privilege that I hold in the highest regard.

It is time to turn the page to a new and exciting chapter in your life. Let's go!

A Heartfelt Intention

May this book and every word in it, give you the *courage to be* …

- you
- seen
- heard
- understood
- appreciated
- loved
- celebrated
- valued
- successful
- magnetic
- dynamic
- admired
- charismatic
- prosperous
- remarkable
- influential
- powerful
- … whatever you want to be

Mind

Having the *courage to be* who you want to be and live a bigger, better life, starts with thinking bigger and better.

Here are some ways for you to do that.

The Life-Changing Magic of 'I'

Ask yourself if what you are doing today is getting you closer to where you want to be tomorrow.

Paulo Coehlo, *Brazilian lyricist and novelist*

It was clear my life was not where I wanted it to be. I was in my late teens, standing on the balcony of my family home, smoking a cigarette for breakfast, and living a life centred around drugs and partying.

I had been kicked out of school and was pursuing a career in hairdressing to keep my parents happy. "If you are not going back to school, you have to work," said my dad. Mission accomplished.

That morning on the balcony, I decided it was time to change and, with a new intention firmly embedded, I trusted life would show me the way forward. I went back to school and finished my high school certificate. Soon afterwards, a friend suggested I intern at an exclusive health retreat. I took their advice, applied and was accepted, not realising how much my life was about to be transformed.

Unlike other health retreats that exist to pamper, this was a place where highly successful, wealthy, influential individuals went to face their demons. Whether they were physical or psychological challenges, you were at this retreat because you wanted to change. No sugar, alcohol, caffeine, drugs, meat, media, mobile phones, porn, you name it, was allowed on the premises – a significant departure from the life I mentioned above.

As an intern, you participated in the program, then worked in each area of the retreat. There was no sitting on the sidelines watching clients undergo their transformations; you were expected to experience change for yourself. The program consisted of tai chi at sunrise, a jog through the rainforest before breakfast, yoga, intense physical activities, group counselling, and one-on-one therapy. I hit pillows, screamed into the ether, pushed my body to the limit, and connected with individuals on a level I didn't even know existed.

Magic happens when we open ourselves up to it.

The person who walked out of the retreat was not the person who'd arrived there. When I returned, I let go of all my party-going friends, began studying Public Relations (PR), and would go on to launch my PR consultancy. My mission at the time was to help spread the word about wellness and personal development. I had experienced firsthand how dramatically things can change when you have the courage to change the things you do, and I wanted to help inspire others to do the same.

I would go on to experience many more life changes, perhaps not so dramatic but just as meaningful. I am sure if we were to sit down together and I had the opportunity to hear your story, the same would apply to you. Change is inevitable and magic happens when we open ourselves up to it.

A big part of this journey is about having the *courage to be* open to change. You are reading this book because you know you are meant for bigger things, and I promise you the world is waiting. It all starts with you and how you use the word 'I'. Let me explain.

After my time at the health retreat, I continued to practise yoga. When I went on extended maternity leave, I made yoga my vocation. I attended classes every day and came to depend on it as my quiet time away from my busy life with 2 very active baby boys. The moment my body landed on the mat, my mind slowed and everything relaxed. Each class would start and end with the chant 'om', a sound that touches me every time I hear it.

Mystics worldwide believe that 'om' is the sound of creation and anyone who chants it is transported into a meditative state where they can better connect with the universe. Numerous studies have supported the health, wellbeing and cognitive benefits this magical sound offers. To me, this only proves that what we say, the sound we create, and the symbolic meaning we associate with what we say, impacts us in more ways than one.

If the sound 'om' represents the essence of life and is a portal to the collective universe, then the sound 'I' represents our world and the universe within. It is one word, one sound, which can change and transform our lives when used correctly; or it can hold us back, trapping us in limited beliefs, ideas and thinking.

I see this principle come to life whenever I begin working with clients. Phrases like, *I am just not like that,* *I have always been that way*, and *I would never be able to do that* hold them back from reaching for the life they want. My mentor has always said: *Keep your word impeccable.* There is no denying that what you say about yourself will impact your reality.

This is why, as we journey towards the life we want to have and the person we want to be, we must first face our unhelpful thoughts, ideas and beliefs about ourselves. We must confront who we think we are, question whether our ideas work for us, then consciously decide who we want to be.

Next time you hear yourself say 'I', listen closely to what follows and ask yourself: Is this belief or statement creating the future I want? Start to think of any 'I' statement as a vote for who you want to be. Become open to the fact that you can start changing your votes by changing your statements (or 'i'ffirmations', as I like to call them). What you say after 'I' will become firmly imbedded in your reality. To change your life and identity, you need to start changing the way you use 'I'.

Recommended Exercise: Audit of 'I'

Have a pen and piece of blank paper ready to go.

Set a timer for 2 minutes and press start.

List as many 'I' statements that come to mind. With time pressure, you won't have time to think, which is ideal. We're looking for your automatic statements. For example: I love nature, I am an introvert, I am a speaker, etc.

When your time is up, review the list and ask yourself the following 3 questions, 1) Is this a fact? 2) Is this statement serving me? 3) If not, what statement will serve me better?

Create a list of 'i-ffirmations' that resonate with the life and person you want to be. These might include:

- I am capable of achieving my goals.
- I am constantly growing and evolving.
- I am in control of my own growth.
- I am open to learning and self-discovery.
- I welcome challenges as opportunities for growth.
- I am committed to my personal development.
- I am becoming the best version of myself.
- I attract positive opportunities for growth.
- I am resilient and capable of overcoming obstacles.

- I believe in my abilities.
- I love the person I am and the person I am becoming.
- I have the power to create my own destiny.
- I choose to focus on progress, not perfection.
- I forgive myself for my mistakes and learn from them.
- I embrace my unique qualities and celebrate who I am.
- I trust myself to make decisions that align with my highest good.
- I am worthy of love and respect.
- I strive to do my best every day, and that's enough.
- I learn something valuable from every experience.
- I am grateful for the opportunities in my life.
- I choose to let go of what no longer serves me.
- I am open to new ideas and perspectives that can help me grow.
- I appreciate my uniqueness and embrace it fully.
- I am dedicated to my journey of personal growth.
- I face challenges with enthusiasm and determination.
- I see mistakes as learning experiences that propel me forward.
- I attract success and prosperity through my efforts.
- I trust the process of life and its timing for me.

- I am capable of creating meaningful connections with others.
- I honour my feelings and allow myself to express them freely.
- I am proactive in seeking opportunities for self-improvement.
- I celebrate my progress, no matter how small it may seem.
- I am a lifelong learner, always seeking knowledge and wisdom.

Make Space for Grace

Life is not merely a series of meaningless accidents or coincidences, but rather a tapestry of events that culminate in an exquisite sublime plan.

Serendipity (2001) *popular film*

I have always believed in magic but not the kind that involves pulling a rabbit out of a hat or performing a disappearing act. I am referring to those curious coincidences that leave even the most cynical person questioning the uncanny timing.

It is the magic found in the moments you think of someone, then suddenly find their name popping up on your phone. Or when you begin contemplating a new beginning and, out of nowhere, you bump into the perfect person to help you take the next step. Magical experiences like these leave a subtle mark on us if we pay attention. You might experience goosebumps, the result of tiny muscles flexing in your skin, hairs raised at the back of your neck, or you may even feel a sudden intuitive nudge in the pit of your belly. In that moment, your body is letting you know you are aligned to the 'exquisite sublime plan', as described in the popular movie *Serendipity*.

Sometimes these magical moments are easy to miss; others are so obvious that life basically offers you a signpost to your goals and dreams. What matters, in both instances, is that you are aware enough to see, hear and recognise those moments. To do that we have to make space for grace and never stop believing in seemingly impossible possibilities that may just be coming our way.

The Oxford Dictionary defines *'grace'* as a divinely given talent or blessing. Irrespective of your religious beliefs, this kind of magic is on offer to us all and can bring a monumental sense of relief. Making space for grace is recognising you don't have to know all the answers or see all the steps ahead. It is about inviting and accepting magical moments to help you along the way.

> *Making space for grace is recognising*
> *you don't have to know all the answers*
> *or see all the steps ahead.*

My entire career in PR came about because of a magical moment of grace.

Twenty years young and recently returned home from a two-month internship at an exclusive health retreat, I was invited to a wellness seminar by a friend. The speaker was bestselling author and human behavioural specialist, Dr John Demartini.

I sat at the back of the seminar room mesmerised. It wasn't just Dr Demartini's magnetic presence, it was the way every word pierced the very centre of my being. I resonated with everything he spoke about and felt destiny had led me to the event. At the end of the session, I quickly rushed over to the merchandise table and purchased a copy of *The Breakthrough Experience* to have it personally signed. I was Dr Demartini's new biggest fan.

Walking out of the venue and into the afternoon sunshine, reflecting on all I had learned, I looked down at my new book and made the decision there and then that I would find a way to work for Dr Demartini. I didn't know how. All I knew was his work was profound, and I wanted as many people as possible to experience everything that I had.

As if on cue, my eyes locked in on the publisher's logo. I felt an intuitive nudge in the pit of my belly. That, I thought, would be my first step. Hay House Australia was about to hear from me or, as it turned out, I would hear from them, in the most remarkable way.

> *What matters is that you are open enough to see, hear and recognise these [magical] moments.*

Armed with the conviction that I had to find a way to work with Dr Demartini, I updated my resumé, wrote a heartfelt covering letter, printed it all out and posted it to Hay House Australia. Email was not a thing to do back then. My resumé was sent, and the waiting game began.

With patience not one of my greatest virtues, I called several times to make sure my resumé had arrived. Each time, I was politely reminded that if there was any interest or opportunity, someone in the team would call me back. I was young enough not to immediately jump to the conclusion that my chances were slim. I continued to wait and did not lose hope. I remained optimistic, though I could never have guessed what would come next.

Months passed then, out of nowhere, I received a call. It was Leon Nacson, Managing Director of Hay House Australia, asking me to come and see him. Most people would question why the Managing Director was calling me, given my status and lack of experience. In all my excitement, I didn't give this a second thought. A date and time were set. I couldn't wait.

When I arrived at Hay House Australia, I was ushered into Leon's office and greeted by his infectious smile and dynamic energy. Famous for wearing slippers to work and never dressing up, Leon has a trademark ability to put a person immediately at ease. Any nervousness I felt quickly evaporated, to be replaced by a sense of awe and amazement.

Leon explained that Dr Demartini was only one of many authors Hay House represented, and that he didn't have any job opportunities to offer. He admitted he was about to go on tour with another high-profile international author so had been tidying up his office. At the very moment he'd picked up my printed resumé to add to the growing pile of recycling, the announcer on the radio playing in the background said, *'And here comes Carly!'* Leon took that as a sign we had to meet.

I will never know who the radio announcer was referring to. All I do know is, in that moment, Leon made space for grace, and I benefited from it. I didn't get a job that day, but Leon was the person who recommended I study PR, then found me my first work experience opportunity at one of Australia's top PR agencies.

When the time was right, Leon introduced me to Dr Demartini, and I managed to sign him as one of my first PR clients. My dream came true, and I gained a lifelong mentor in Leon – all because we both made space for grace. Leon refers to this as The Conspiracy of Improbability, a term I have grown to love.

When you think ahead to your dreams and goals, ask yourself: what is possible when I make space for grace?

I am confident the answer will be ... anything!

Embrace What You DK

The more that you read, the more things you will know.
The more that you learn, the more places you'll go.

Dr. Seuss, *author and cartoonist*

It is amazing how important life lessons can come when you least expect them. This lesson came to me while feeding my children breakfast.

I asked my youngest son, Alessandro, what he wanted to eat, and he replied, "DK." Bewildered and wondering if I had missed the purchase of a new strangely branded cereal, I quickly asked what he meant. To which he said, with a cheeky grin, "Don't know."

I laughed out loud; it was a timely reminder of how quickly things change; even the way we communicate changes over time. Anyone with teenage children can tell you that with each generation comes an entirely new language and set of terms. I later reflected how important it is to keep learning, and that with change comes confusion. Learning new things applies to every area of life and any worthwhile endeavour.

If who you are today reflects all that you know, then the life you want to live may be on the other side of all that you don't yet know. Change brings with it the invitation to learn new things and, in doing so, we DK what new opportunities will emerge. I have the perfect story to bring this lesson to life.

> *If who you are today reflects all that you know, then the life you want to live may be on the other side of all that you don't yet know.*

I remember watching her enter the room. Her hair was the kind of blonde that doesn't come naturally, and she wore heavy eye make-up. Despite the fact that she was tiny, she had magnetic energy and charisma that no one could deny.

We were sitting next to one another at a seminar hosted by my client, Dr John Demartini. She was there because she was in the process of creating a documentary and wanted to interview him as part of it. I was there because I was his hired gatekeeper and wanted to explore whether the documentary was worthwhile for Dr Demartini.

She had been a television producer with a major network, then, after her father died, she had fallen into a deep depression. While searching for a way out, she discovered the world of personal development and spirituality. She wanted to share the new things she had learned and decided to use her professional skills to do so. She had connections and professional credibility as a producer, but no background in the personal development space.

The documentary was *The Secret* and the lady's name was Rhonda Byrne. In 2007, Rhonda would go on to be featured in *Time* magazine as one of the most influential people in the world. Her book, based on the earlier film of the same name, sold 30 million copies worldwide and was translated into 50 languages. Learning something new led her to a completely different life.

When you embrace what you don't know and remain open to discovering new things, you uncover new parts of yourself. In doing so, doors open to new ways and new places you didn't know existed.

The problem is that most people don't have the *courage to be* a beginner and see their lack of knowledge as proof they are venturing down the wrong path. At this point, we would all be wise to embrace the words of Robin Sharma, bestselling Canadian author, who said: *Every master was once a beginner. Every pro was once an amateur.*

Being a beginner and learning new things means we will make mistakes, but we accept that it comes hand in hand with being a learner for life. The more you embrace what you don't know, the more you learn. And the more you learn, the more you grow. What something new can you learn this week?

Speak Back to the Little You

Words have the power to harm us, especially when they come from the voice in our heads.

Anonymous

Early in my career, I believed in myself in all the wrong ways. I believed what my little voice said, and I can recall countless moments and experiences where it led me to play small. One instance comes to mind.

A few years into running my PR consultancy, a popular women's magazine reached out to me and asked if they could profile me as a young woman in business representing amazing clients. It was an opportunity to put myself out there and build my own brand.

I quickly called one of my clients to see if they would be happy for me to go ahead with the interview. I didn't have to ask my clients for permission, but I was so desperate for someone to tell me I was good enough, I needed that assurance. My little voice was shouting, *You're not good enough. You don't know what you are doing. They will find out you are a fraud!*

I didn't go ahead with the interview. I let my small voice win.

I trusted that those negative messages about myself were the truth. Today, looking back, it makes me all the more determined to never let that happen again.

> *I believed what my little voice said, and*
> *I can recall countless moments and*
> *experiences where it led me to play small.*

Here is a scary thought: the average person has up to 60,000 thoughts per day. Of those thoughts, 80% are negative and 95% were the same as the day before! Not only are we recycling the same thoughts over and over, most of the time they are negative.

As you read this book, you will be increasingly aware of the benefits and virtues of positive thinking, but I am not going to tell you to think positive all the time. Why? Because too much positive thinking can be negative. Even I struggle to trust a person who seems to be always upbeat and happy. It doesn't feel genuine. As humans, we are here to experience the full spectrum of emotions, and with that comes a delectable selection of thoughts: some good, some bad, and even some that are outright nasty.

The aim is not about ridding ourselves of all bad thoughts or banishing negativity from our minds; instead, there is a strategy I have found that is much more powerful and realistic. It can be perfectly illustrated in a story about the famous operatic tenor, Caruso.

As the story goes, Caruso was backstage, preparing to go on stage and deliver a very important career performance. Out of nowhere, his vocal cords began to seize up and he was convinced the show could not go on. Caruso anxiously paced back and forth behind the curtain, while the crowd rumbled in anticipation. He knew he had to make a decision quickly.

Nervous and shaking, he screamed out, "They will laugh at me. I can't sing." Then he shouted, while others were watching on, "The Little Me wants to strangle the Big Me within." He said, "Get out of here, the Big Me wants to sing through me." Caruso then went on stage and gave the performance of a lifetime.

Long story short, Caruso spoke back to the little voice within.

Call it the little voice, the inner critic, call it whatever you like. Dr Carol Dweck, a Stanford psychologist and author of the international bestseller, *Mindset*, suggests that giving the little voice a name helps. It allows you to create distance and take control of what thoughts you act on and what thoughts you speak back to.

As you work with this process, you'll find it is easy to hear the difference between these voices. Your little voice will do everything it can to keep you thinking, acting and being small. It is the voice that tells you not to put yourself out there, not to share your ideas, not to speak up and allow yourself to be heard. It is the voice that tells you the dreams you have are not realistic, and certainly not possible for someone like you.

On the flipside, your big voice reminds you that you can be, do and have everything you want. It reminds you that your dreams are important. It is the voice that whispers to you that you really are here to achieve great things. It is inspiring, uplifting, powerful and expansive. It is the voice you want to listen to, and the only way to make it louder is to give it the proverbial microphone. I wish I had learned these insights at the beginning of my career.

The takeaway? Don't wait for the future to learn this lesson. Talk back to the little voice within. I promise that when you do, big things will start to happen.

Quieten Your Inner Drama Queen (or King)

Drama starts where logic ends.

Ram Charan, *Indian actor and film producer*

I was no longer good enough to be her friend; she had changed, and not in a good way, and it was time to let go and accept that our friendship had ended. These were only some of the destructive thoughts my Inner Drama Queen (IDQ) was trying to convince me of. There is what happens to us in life, then there's what we tell ourselves has happened. Often, without us consciously deciding what we believe, our IDQ or Inner Drama King (IDK) takes over and turns a molehill into a mountain.

As a former international personal publicist, it was my role to embellish the truth and spin a story to be as positive or negative as possible, depending on the intention. I was pretty good at what I did, but even I am an amateur compared to my IDQ.

The thoughts mentioned above all started because a friend hadn't called me back. Let me give you an amusing example of my IDQ in action, so you can save yourself from the same kind of drama in your life.

*There is what happens to us in life, then there's
what we tell ourselves has happened.*

I have a friend I have known since high school. We do not see each other often, but I have always had a soft spot for her. She is incredibly likeable, down to earth, and one of those rare individuals who can make anyone feel comfortable in her presence. We both had babies around the same time, and I remember her coming over for a play date to tell me about a business idea she had to help mums get back in shape after having babies.

Fast-forward to today, and she has created a fitness empire. She has been featured on the covers of magazines and has launched her business internationally. I could not be happier for her, and it is so exciting to witness her success.

Even with all this said, my IDQ was able to turn this beautiful friend of mine into a foe. Here is how it unfolded in my mind.

I had a business opportunity related to the world of health and fitness, and I knew this friend would be perfect to speak with. Given she had been so busy building her empire, we had not spoken for a while. Instead of calling, I decided to send a message and make time to see her in person. I waited patiently for a reply.

A few weeks later, and still no response, my IDQ went into overdrive and had me starting to think the worst. My frustration mounted as the days passed and I was convinced my friend was intentionally ignoring me.

That was until I received a message from her husband apologising on her behalf and letting me know her grandmother, whom she loved dearly, was close to death. My friend had stopped everything to spend the last precious moments with a woman who had shaped her life in every way.

My heart broke for my dear friend; all I wanted to do was hug her.

Beyond my initial shock, I took the time to become aware of the crazy thoughts I had entertained, all because I had not received a message back. This was the work of my IDQ, whose response was pointless and potentially damaging.

We can all let our imaginations get the better of us and create scenarios in our minds that are negative. As much as we might say that is just how we are, it is not the truth. We can control our minds and put our IDQ in its place. This is an important habit to master on the path to putting yourself out there and becoming more visible. Imaginary drama can end with us giving up, making the wrong decisions, and being too scared to pursue opportunities and relationships.

In my own life, I have found the following 3 actions help me bring about a new perspective and keep centred in truth:

1. **Put pen to paper and write it all out** – the conspiracy theories, stories and excuses that are circling in your mind. Most of the time, you will see how ridiculous they are. By writing it out, you give permission for your rational mind to take over and put your IDQ or IDK in its place.

2. **Give your imagined story a positive spin** – instead of simply going along for the crazy ride my IDQ was taking me on, I had the option to stop and create other possible reasons my friend had not got back to me. These could have included that she was busy brokering an international deal or travelling in a different time zone. If you are going to make up a story, why not make sure it is positive and one that makes you feel good?

3. **Go with the flow** – I went from feeling offended to upset and angry, all because my IDQ wanted to create drama. I could have easily said to myself that she would get back to me at the perfect time, which would have been the end of the matter. Life unfolds as it is meant to.

What happens in your mind is the difference between a simple life and a complicated one. Drama is a choice and one that is not worthwhile. You will never know what someone else thinks of you or what the future holds. Why not believe in the best and trust in the timing of life?

We all fear the unknown to some degree, and drama is our way of filling in the blanks. So, let's fill the blanks with stories of love, hope and gratitude. If you make something up, do it to make you feel good.

Sure, our IDQ or IDK may come in handy when writing the script of that Academy Award-winning movie script, but other than that, let go of the drama and keep it simple. What drama can you let go of this week?

Stop Learning, Start Doing

Nothing will work unless you do.

Maya Angelou, *writer and civil rights activist*

Despite my academic record as a high school dropout, I do love to learn. I love anything related to personal and professional development, with a vast book collection to prove it. In the early days of my PR career, I was fortunate enough to represent and work with many well-known speakers, experts and authors in the personal development industry. This meant I also had the privilege of attending many events and workshops for free.

Like any industry, once you are in it, you realise how small and interconnected it is. You also start to see lots of familiar faces, and not always in a good way. The crowd I am referring to here were known as the 'self-help junkies'. These were the individuals you could depend on to be at every event. They would leave you questioning whether they were putting any of this learning into action. It was as if attending the event was progress enough for them. Learning had become a substitute for doing the work.

I see this same mentality in my clients in a slightly different way. When they decide it is time to aim for the next level of their career, they automatically assume they will need another certificate, degree or PhD. In some cases, this is wise and makes sense, in others it is a flamboyant form of procrastination.

Rather than learning more, they need to do more. In the international bestselling book, *What They Don't Teach You at Harvard Business School*, author and founder of IMG, Mark H McCormack writes: I do not have an innate prejudice against intellect, intelligence or, for that matter, graduate degrees, but they are not substitutes for common sense, people sense and street smarts. In many instances, I also believe my clients need to work on developing their people skills, intuitive instincts and leadership abilities through life experience and doing the work.

Reading, researching and learning all play a vital part in our development, but they don't replace the important step of doing the work. How we do the work means different things to different people. For some, it is creating the product they have been dreaming of, writing the book they have been ruminating over, pitching the idea they have been developing in their minds, or having the courage to put themselves out there and build their profile.

In her book *Grit*, psychologist Angela Duckworth recounts a story that sums this up perfectly. During a weekly meeting with her academic adviser, who happened to be psychology icon Martin Seligman, they discussed the progress she was making in developing new ideas. He offered her this unexpected and uncomfortable advice: *"Stop reading so much and go think."* In this case, thinking was the work she needed to do.

> *Stop reading so much and go think.*

In my coaching sessions, I have also come across the misguided belief that studying more will increase self-confidence. I have not found this to be true. The feeling of confidence does not come from knowing more, it comes from taking confident action and doing more.

One client admitted they hoped more certificates - and even a master's degree -would help them overcome the fear they felt when putting themselves out there. They were aspiring to be an international speaker and author but were afraid when it came to sharing their ideas and thought leadership with the world. In this case, my client's life experience mattered more than academic theories, but learning more had become an elaborate method of avoiding the work they knew they had to do.

When I first launched myself as a personal branding coach, I created business cards that featured the following quote: *There are people less qualified than you, doing the things you want to do simply because they decide to believe in themselves. Period.* This quote was as much a reminder to myself as it was to the clients I worked with and the people I met along the way.

> *There are people less qualified than you, doing the things you want to do simply because they decide to believe in themselves. Period.*

There will always be opportunities to learn and grow. It is important to stay open to that, but don't let it stop you from acting in the now and doing the work you can do today. Only you know if learning has become a delaying tactic. Instead of ordering another book or taking another course, what confident step can you take towards your dreams?

Channel the Power of Your Attention

The eyes do not see what the mind does not want.
Indian proverb

There is a beautiful quote by Henry David Thoreau, writer and philosopher, which goes: *It is not what you look at that matters, it is what you see.* As a philosopher, I am not sure how familiar Thoreau was with neuroscience, but his statement is also true on a scientific level.

Though we want to believe everything is as we see it when we see it, the truth is what we see is dependent on who we are and what we choose to pay attention to.

In *Mind Magic*, Stanford neurosurgeon, Dr James Doty, writes: Our system is bombarded by about ten million bits of data per second, the equivalent of ten HD movies. However, it is able to process only about fifty bits consciously. This means that about 99.9995 percent of our brains' bandwidth is not available to our conscious mind. Doty goes on to suggest we need to create healthier habits of attention and actively program our subconscious mind to know what is important to us.

*What we see depends on
what we are looking for.*

A quick and easy way to experience the power of this insight is to ask yourself the following question: How many red things can I see right now? Then scan the room or place you are in.

Did you notice the way your attention zoomed in on everything that was red. In that moment, you consciously took control of your attention and directed your brain to scan for what you wanted. It seems the childhood game of 'I spy' was teaching us an important life lesson we can use to our advantage. What we see depends on what we are looking for.

Firsthand, I have seen clients go from thinking their personal brand doesn't matter, to flipping the switch and saying: *I have a personal brand and what I have to offer is important.* Almost instantaneously, they begin to see and receive opportunities to build their profile and put themselves out there.

The opportunities were always there, but their belief system and habits of attention meant my clients couldn't *see* them. The great news is there are very practical steps you can take today to make sure those opportunities are not getting lost in your internal filters.

Start with the following actions:

- **Write out your goals** and keep them somewhere you can access them daily. This will ensure your subconscious mind is programmed to scan your environment for ways to make your goals a reality.

- **Set a recurring reminder in your diary each week** with the question: What steps am I taking this week to achieve my goals? Questions let your subconscious mind know what information and ideas to pay attention to.

- **Visualise what success looks like** and focus on that image whenever you can. Think of this as a way of teaching your subconscious mind how to make your dreams a reality. The more you practice, the more you wire your system to scan, see and zoom in on the things that can help you achieve your vision of success.

> *The opportunities were always there, but their belief system and habits of attention meant they couldn't see them.*

Attention is a form of currency. Where we **pay** attention will dictate the return on investment we get in our life and career. Our attention is a limited resource that deserves to be closely guarded and carefully nurtured. If what we see and pay attention to depends solely on who we are and how we have programmed our subconscious minds, then the power and control is in our hands (and minds).

Don't allow your attention to be hijacked. Take steps to take control of what you pay attention to and, in doing so, chances are you will see a whole new world in front of you.

Remember, the opportunities to be seen, heard and known are out there, but the question is: Are you? And, more importantly: Can you see these opportunities?

Turn Memories into Mojo

Life happens for you, not to you.

Byron Katie, *speaker and writer*

I am eternally fascinated by the random things I remember. If we all had a secretary living in our heads who was responsible for what gets filed in the 'to remember' pile, I would seriously need to talk to my internal HR department and whoever oversees which memories I recall!

Like most people, I always thought of memories as things. Factual recollections of thoughts, images, feelings, smells and even tastes that remained static and unchanged over time. How I remembered a thing was clearly how it happened, and it was not open to interpretation … or so I thought.

It seems my thinking on this topic was as distorted as many of the memories I have. The truth is most memories are a mix of fact and fiction. Our memories change as we change, and I am not referring to memory loss due to old age. We embellish, selectively edit and manipulate our memories of the past to suit and reinforce who we are in the present.

In the *Journal of Neuroscience*, Donna Bridge, postdoctoral fellow at Northwestern University Feinberg School of Medicine, was quoted as saying: Your memory of an event can grow less precise even to the point of being totally false with each retrieval. A scary thought worth remembering word for word!

In *Time and Psychological Explanation*, psychologist Dr Brent Slife states: We reinterpret or reconstruct our memory in light of what our mental set is in the present. In this sense, it is more accurate to say the present causes the meaning of the past, than it is to say that the past causes the meaning of the present. Our memories are not 'stored' and 'objective' entities but living parts of ourselves in the present. This is the reason our present moods and future goals so affect our memories.

> *It is more accurate to say the present*
> *causes the meaning of the past,*
> *than it is to say that the past causes*
> *the meaning of the present.*

When I first came across this line of research and thinking, I couldn't help but do a mental spring-clean of the memories that were holding me back. I realised I had been shapeshifting my memories in a way that was working against me. Let me give you an example.

I studied PR at college and while I was there, I met a guy who I will call James for the purpose of this book. James was in his 40s and had a boutique marketing agency. He specialised in helping companies run outlandish competitions. If you have ever seen promotions that offer unbelievable prizes like 'win your own island', that is the kind of thing James did. He was at college studying PR to add to his professional skill set.

During break one day, James and I started chatting and in no time at all he had offered me a part-time job. I was hired to help with business development, and it was my role to get James in front of big brands. I was successful in setting up meetings with brands like L'Oréal and Pfizer, but quickly realised the role was not for me.

Feeling bad about letting him down, but sure I was making the right decision, I broke the news to James. After the meeting, as I stood to leave, James said in a cold, almost emotionless tone, "You look better than you actually are." I left feeling winded.

Being young and impressionable, I walked away and turned the memory of that unfortunate encounter into a belief system that haunted me and my career for many years to come. I bought into the idea that perhaps I did look more confident and capable than I really was.

This was one of the first memories that was put through my spring-cleaning process. I began to look at this painful incident from a different perspective. James should have known better than to put me down so completely. I now realise he reacted that way because he was not able to keep a talented young operator in his fledgling marketing business. His comments reflected his own insecurities, not mine. From this new and empowered perspective, I saw a bright young woman taking control of her time and future by making the right decisions. I saw a guy frustrated by his own limitations. I took control of the narrative, and, with that, I took my power back. Now it is your turn.

Take the time to think about, and write out, some of the memories you feel are holding you back. These will be the ones that seem to pop up whenever you are about to decide to step outside of your comfort zone. Knowing your memories are a mix of fact and fiction, how can you use the memory for good? What are the positive lessons that will put the power back in your lap?

They say: *The best things in life are the people you love, the places you go, and the memories you make.* There is no deadline for making those memories; you always have the power to go back and make them work for you. What memory can you change today?

Trust Your Intuition Always

Gut feelings are guardian angels.

Anonymous

As improbable as it sounds, one nagging intuitive thought that was followed by a heartfelt email helped me save the life of a loved one. If you have ever questioned the importance of listening to your intuition, I suggest you learn from my lesson. It all started from a place of serious hunger.

Over a decade ago, I embarked on a trip to Koh Samui in Thailand to experience a 10-day fast. Some might say it was a long way to travel to eat nothing; however, this spa was renowned all around the world for its detox programs.

Several friends warned me it could end up being quite an emotional experience. Not so much emotional because you are crying on the inside from hunger – emotional because when you detox your physical body, you detox your emotional body as well.

I was prepared for the worst and explained to close friends and family that I would not be contactable over the 10-day period. I wanted to focus on myself and tune in to everything I was thinking and feeling. I packed a journal, a pen, and not much else. There would be no television, no cell phones and no reminders of the outside world.

The spa was situated in the remote mountains of Koh Samui and as soon as I arrived, I loved everything about the place. It was not luxurious or pretentious. The accommodation was very basic, but the surroundings were exotic. I had a private cabin at the top of a hill surrounded by lush jungle (not great on Day 4 of the fast), and I felt as though I was a world away from everything (especially food!).

My friends were right about my emotions. They ran wild. Up until Day 4, I found myself replaying things in my past that I had buried long ago. While my surroundings were the epitome of peace and quiet, my internal mental landscape was anything but. On Day 5, my mind calmed down and a sense of serenity washed over me.

That is when it happened. Suddenly, out of nowhere, I got a nagging intuitive feeling that I needed to contact a certain loved one. I could not shake this. I kept trying to convince myself I was just missing home, but this prompting did not stop. Every time I thought of this person, I felt heavy, and all I could see was black.

Resigned to the fact I would not stop thinking about this until I did something about it, I made the long journey to the spa's reception and sent an email. My intuition had taken me to that point, so I decided to leave it up to my intuition to determine what I would write.

My email went on to tell this person how much I loved them, that I could not envisage my life without them, and that I would always be there whenever they needed me. I reminded them that being grateful for what you have and focusing on the good is one way to get through a challenging moment and keep hope alive.

I had not been in contact with this person for some time, but I wrote what I felt intuitively needed to be said. A few days later I received a response I will never forget.

My loved one explained they were feeling so down they had considered taking their own life. The day they seriously contemplated acting on that fatal idea was the day they received my email. It changed the course of their life, as indeed their response changed the course of mine.

On receiving that return email, I learned the importance of trusting your intuition even when it doesn't make sense.

Albert Einstein, famous physicist, was quoted as saying: *The intuitive mind is a sacred gift and the rational mind a faithful servant. We have created a society that honours the servant and has forgotten the gift.* How true this is. Your intuition is the gift that keeps giving; the more you listen to it, the stronger it becomes. In this case, listening to my intuition was literally a matter of life or death.

Perhaps, for you, having the courage to listen to your intuition won't be a matter of life or death, but it will greatly contribute to your creating the life you want to lead. When you have an intuitive nudge to do something, reach out to someone, ask for an opportunity, or even say 'yes' to an unexpected invitation, trust it. You never know where it might lead or what doors it might open.

According to AI (Artificial Intelligence), here are 5 ways to develop your AI (Actual Intuition). Keep in mind that the word 'actual' is defined by the Oxford Dictionary as *existing in fact/real*.

1. **Meditation**: Regular meditation can help you clear your mind of distractions and recognise subtle impulses. It can also help you balance options objectively and make rational and intuitive decisions.

2. **Dream work**: Interpreting your dreams can help you connect with your intuition. Dreams can bridge the conscious and unconscious mind, where intuition is located.

3. **Body scans**: Notice how different parts of your body are feeling throughout the day. This can help you recognise when your intuition is trying to get your attention.

4. **Journaling**: Keeping an intuition journal can help you increase your trust in your intuition.

5. **Asking questions**: Asking questions can help you challenge your assumptions and consider new perspectives.

They say your intuition is whispers from the soul. What has your soul been whispering to you lately? Importantly, have you been listening?

Talk To Your Future Self Regularly

Human beings are works in progress that mistakenly think they are finished.

Dr Daniel Gilbert, *social psychologist and writer*

When I ask clients if they are the same person they were 5 years ago, the most common answer I get is 'no'. Looking back over our past, it is easy to see how we have changed as individuals. Yet according to research, we tend to underestimate how much we will change in the future.

To make the point, Harvard psychologist, Dr Daniel Gilbert, coined the term *'end of history illusion'*. This explains the psychological illusion individuals have when they get to a point in their life and think they are unlikely to experience any further significant changes. They believe they are who they are, and, other than physically ageing, they will remain the same. A dangerous illusion indeed.

Rather than assume we will remain the same, there is real power in accepting that our future self is going to be a different person altogether. By keeping this top of mind, our thoughts and actions remain future-focused and open-minded.

This is further explored in the work and research of another pioneer in the world of 'future self' psychology, Dr Hal Hershfield. In his TEDx talk titled *How Can We Help Our Future Selves?* Hershfield suggests there is power in closing the gap between our current self and our future self by *"starting a conversation"*. This, he suggests, might be through *"writing a vivid letter to your distant self"* or *"downloading an age progressed image and putting it somewhere in your house where you regularly make long-term decisions"*. The idea being that, by closing the gap, *"we can start making better decisions today that brighten tomorrow"*.

Though it can be hard to imagine, if we are blessed to live a long life, we will one day all grow old. We will undoubtedly have wisdom to share, and, with a little imagination, I don't think we have to wait to close the gap and tap into that wisdom our future self has to offer.

Perhaps our past self does not have the answers we are looking for at any given moment. What if we were to look to our future self for the solution? What if we were to try to consider how our older, wiser self might look upon a situation? Sure, guesswork and storytelling are involved, but even our recollection of the past can be at the mercy of our storytelling ways.

When I tune into my distant future self, here are some of the most important messages she has to offer me (and now you) …

You are beautiful

Enjoy your youth and beauty, every single ounce of it. You are full of life until your heart stops beating. We live in a society with a warped definition of what beauty is. We have been sold the idea that beauty ends as soon as we begin to see any minor signs of ageing. Each season of life brings changes with it. When you embrace those changes for what they represent, you emanate the kind of beauty and confidence that goes beyond the physical. Celebrate your unique form of beauty and have the courage to flaunt it right until the end.

If you can move it, use it

Moving, jumping, swimming, stretching, dancing, running, hopping, skipping and walking are among the most precious gifts of living. As simple as each may sound, they offer so much genuine joy and freedom. How many times in a day are you grateful to be able to walk freely? If not at least once, you are under the illusion that time cannot take away this simple yet profoundly important gift. Take care of your body. Enjoy moving it as much as possible and never take it for granted.

Don't worry about what other people think

Throughout your life, many people will come and go – more than you can contemplate at the beginning of your journey. People you are so eager to please today will be a distant memory in time to come. The only person you will always have with you is **you**. Do what makes you happy, live according to your inner voice, and trust that will create a positive ripple effect in the lives of everyone around you. If all you do is try to make others happy, you will lose touch with what makes you happy.

Family and friends count most

As important as career and achievement is to your sense of self-worth and purpose, in the end, your loved ones will matter most. What you give, you get back. Invest time in nurturing and loving the people you care about. You are never too busy to show them you care. Tell them today, and every day after that, that you love them. Just as time will eventually erode your body, so too will it take away the ones you love. There is no greater regret than to watch a loved one pass and know you never got to say all that was needed to be said. Cherish your loved ones with all your heart and make the most of every moment you share, even all those mundane moments.

Enjoy the journey

What seems like a huge problem today will become a memory in time to come. Your pain, stress, worries and fear will be healed by time and space, if you allow the natural course of life to take its place. Learn to appreciate even the hard times and you will have genuinely mastered life. We are here to experience the entire spectrum of human experience; to expect only light, joy, happiness, fun and success is to be completely deluded. No matter who you are, where you come from, or what you do, you will experience darkness, sadness, failure, boredom, loss and tragedy. Be prepared for the full spectrum of life experiences. When your time comes, knowing all the ups, downs and roundabouts will make sense.

If you ever get stuck in the now or, worse still, in the past, let your future self guide you; do something today that your future self will be grateful for. What would your future self say to you right now?

Try this powerful time travel exercise:

- Find a quiet comfortable place to sit.
- Take a deep breath, inhale/exhale, and then close your eyes.
- Imagine your older future self, picture their aged hands, their weathered body, and see them moving slowly.
- Now invite them to travel back from the future, to live in your body and have a second chance at life.
- Feel them inhabit your youthful body and appreciate the excitement they feel knowing they'll get to do it all again.
- Now open your eyes and see the world from their perspective.

The above exercise is inspired by the work of Dr Benjamin Hardy, author of *Be Your Future Self Now*. When I first experienced this process for myself, I was having a challenging morning. I felt frustrated and angry. My kids were fighting, and my husband had said something that annoyed me.

I sat on the end of my bed, closed my eyes, and did the exercise as outlined. A few minutes later, I opened my eyes, and everything felt different. I was grateful that my husband, the man I love so dearly, was still there by my side. I looked at my boys and wanted desperately to stop them from growing up so fast. I knew one day I would miss the craziness of their youth. I knew it because I had been there in the future. In those few quiet minutes, I had given my future self the opportunity to do that present moment all over again. My wiser, older self had helped me to see everything through new eyes. Her eyes.

You can access my free Future Self Guided Meditation by visiting **www.carliilyon.com/futureselfmeditation**

Think About Your Funeral Everyday

*Dying is easy. Life is hard ...
but ridiculously rewarding. Challenge yourself.*

Vanessa Juresic, *an inspiration*

I can picture my funeral clearly; I see the faces of the people I love, and I have even selected the music. My husband hates talking about it but knows what I want.

Considering I am a healthy 43-year-old woman, you might think I am a little crazy. But contemplating the end helps me cherish the present. It offers a vital reminder to be grateful for the good times, gives me strength to get through the hard times, and helps me make better decisions for the future.

Whether it is our own end, or bearing witness to someone else's, death can transform the way we see and experience life. Here is a story that perfectly illustrates what I mean.

One Saturday morning some time back, I bumped into a long-lost friend, Lisa, on the sideline of our children's local soccer game. After a quick catch-up on all things to do with family, career and life in general, with tears in her eyes, Lisa shared tragic news about a mutual friend we had during high school. Vanessa was dying of cancer.

I had heard through the grapevine that Vanessa was ill, but had assumed, given she was young, there was a good chance she would get better. Sadly, I learned that there was very little hope for Vanessa, and it was only a matter of time before her passing. As we stood on the muddy sidelines, reflecting on the fragility of life, suddenly the hordes of screaming children around us felt like a true blessing.

Through the pain of it all, Lisa shared how watching her best friend slowly fade away had changed her life. The trivial problems she faced no longer mattered, and she was so grateful for all she had.

I walked away with a heavy heart for Lisa, who was clearly struggling with the pain of it all, and for Vanessa, who faced a seemingly impossible battle ahead. I could only pray they would both find peace in what the future would bring.

> *The trivial problems she faced no longer mattered, and she was so grateful for all she had.*

Months after that fateful encounter on the soccer sidelines with Lisa, I received the news that Vanessa passed away. I decided to attend the funeral. Even though I had lost touch with Vanessa, I wanted to celebrate and pay respect to the bright, funny, caring woman I remembered from all those years ago.

Surrounded by seemingly thousands of people, I sat in the audience and watched Lisa bravely step up to the podium. As a dying wish, Vanessa asked Lisa to read out a letter she had written prior to her death. With little time and strength, prior to passing, Vanessa made sure she had the last word in the most beautiful and impactful way. With permission, I am sharing the letter here in its full form.

> *If you knew me, you know I always wanted to have the last word. I'm sure in most circumstances this was an exceptionally annoying trait, but I'm hoping at times, endearing?*
>
> *Today is no different.*
>
> *Life is so fragile and so beautiful. Never in my worst nightmares would I have ever imagined I would be taken so soon – ripped away from every single beautiful person here.*
>
> *I wanted to be the miracle kid on the front cover of National Geographic, but that wasn't meant to be. Someone up there must need me more for some reason – to look over you all.*
>
> *I had so much more to do. I wanted to join boards, write more policy, and change the world for the better, fundraise more, mentor and 'make a difference' as they say.*
>
> *So, I'm going to give it a go here instead and give you my learnings from my short life.*

What would I have told my pre-cancer self if I knew my end was so near? What would I have appreciated more? What advice would I give to my loved ones?

If you want something, go get it, now – trust me, you don't want to be writing this letter. Stop procrastinating.

There are 3 rules:

- *If you do not go after what you want, you will never have it.*
- *If you do not ask, the answer will always be 'no'.*
- *If you do not step forward, you will remain in the same place.*

And most importantly, my golden rule: In a world where you can be anything ... be kind.

And don't let anyone make you cruel. No matter how badly you want to give the world a taste of its own bitter medicine, it is never worth losing yourself.

You never know what struggle someone is going through in their own lives.

In the past year, I learnt that more than ever. Trivial things which bothered people paled into insignificance while fighting cancer. It made me want to shake people and say, 'If it won't matter in 5 years, don't waste 5 more minutes on it' ... but it's all about perspective and finding my inner kind and understanding got me through that struggle.

In a weird way I consider myself lucky, despite some serious struggles in the past decade. Everything was a lesson and everything made me stronger ... more understanding of people and appreciation of what I do have.

The love and support I got while sick was gobsmacking. The gifts, the money raising, the calls, texts and overall lovefest really helped me get through the journey. I had no idea so many people cared – about me, and my family. Nope. My appreciation will never be able to be put into words but know each act of kindness touched my soul.

We're all impeccably lucky here. We have all had a world-class education, upbringing, and opportunity – so much opportunity. We're in the minority.

I said at my grandmother's funeral that we don't realise it. She had my father in a refugee camp. No fancy private hospital, doctors or drugs. In the '40s you were lucky to graduate from Year 3. I picked my degree out of a glossy mag – the vast gap and obvious opportunity I've been handed is just unreal comparably.

I ate the best food, travelled to the 4 corners of the world, surrounded myself with some of the best humans to ever grace this earth and thrived on a challenging career – what more could a girl want?

Yes, I wanted a family of my own, a long healthy life with the love of my life, Patrick.

More travel, more time to appreciate every Christmas, birthday, Olympics, election, glass of fine wine, bowl of pasta and serve of apple crumble.

But I'm not going to say to you to appreciate all these things in case you die. That's too predictable. Instead, I say don't overanalyse life and fear a horrible fate. Just live your full, wonderful lives and don't give mortality a second thought.

I was unlucky, but you are not.

Terminal or not, you should be reaching for the stars, taking advantage of the amazing life you've been handed. Not because you might die!

Dying is easy. Life is hard ... but ridiculously rewarding. Challenge yourself.

Do that gym session you think you can't do or run that half marathon.

Travel to that random country, challenge your boss.

Girls, smash that glass ceiling and stop trying to fit into glass slippers.

Go for that job – eat that Christmas pudding and enjoy it. Overindulge in happiness – because you're alive, not because you might die.

Don't settle. At work, in that relationship – with anything. Keep fighting to get what you want. The best decisions I made in life weren't easy, but they were the ones where I found the strength to not settle.

And the happiness and sense of achievement I got in return was worth the pain.

I only wish I'd figured this out earlier in life. God always opened up a window when I knew shutting the door was the right thing to do, so trust and this will happen for you too. Don't be scared. Life is short.

I loved people. There are so many extraordinary and complex amazing people to absorb and discover in the world. Notice them.

I hope even today – a day which is traditionally supposed to be a sad day – that I can provide a link, for everyone here.

Be with each other.

Find comfort in each other.

Reach out and touch somebody today. For me. Remember me.

I would have loved nothing more than to be with you all with a cold glass of wine in hand, celebrating life.

Introduce yourself and hug my mum, dad, brother and sister, then go home and hug your family – say hello to someone you don't know today. I guarantee every person here is an amazing individual.

To my family, I was who I was because of you. The love I was afforded was second to none and if only every child was given that kind of stable love, this world would be a better place.

Continue to love each other just as much as I loved every single one of you.

Organise all those annoying dinners I would insist on and remember that family always comes first. At birth, and all the way through to death. We're one.

You've done everything for me. Now focus on you and your lives! We've never seen tragedy like this. Make your bond stronger through it!

Patrick – you made me the happiest I have ever been. You changed my life.

I dreamt of a big, beautiful family with you, to grow old with you and I hate that this insidious disease ripped our dreams away from us.

I'll always be in your soul and you in mine. Nothing can ever take that away from us. Real love stories never end.

To every other single person in this room – each and every one of you touched my life in some special way, and I hope I touched yours too.

Don't forget those moments and notice future moments with each other – they're important. Trust me.

> *Duncan Gay, a former Nationals politician and my old boss, was a man I looked up to. A man who believed in me and mentored me. On his exit from Parliament recently, he quoted Winnie the Pooh, and I couldn't agree more with what he said: "How lucky I am to have something that makes saying goodbye so hard."*
>
> *Thank you for coming today. I hope I'm here in spirit. If there is a way I can look over all of you and give a good word to the big fella I will, particularly when it comes to the Tigers or Man United winning a season.*
>
> *I love you all and miss you already.*
>
> *This isn't goodbye though – it's 'see you soon'.*
>
> *Until we meet again.*

Vanessa's letter would later be shared in the media and ended up going viral. Millions of lives globally were touched, and no doubt changed because of it. Death did not stop Vanessa from making a difference; in fact, I dare say she had the courage to make sure it didn't, and we are all richer for it.

> *Don't settle. At work, in that relationship – with anything. Keep fighting to get what you want. The best decisions I made in life weren't easy, but they were the ones where I found the strength to not settle.*

One of the best books I have ever read is *The Top Five Regrets of the Dying*. Bronnie Ware, a palliative care nurse, recognised the wisdom her patients bestowed in their last days and decided to share it with the world. The top 5 regrets as she presents them are:

I wish I'd had the courage to live a life true to myself, not the life others expected of me.

I wish I hadn't worked so hard.

I wish I'd had the courage to express my feelings.

I wish I had stayed in touch with my friends.

I wish that I had let myself be happier.

After reading the book, I decided to think of my funeral consistently. Not in a gloomy way, but in a way that would remind me to stay present and grateful.

Thinking about the end creates a healthy sense of urgency. It offers an important reminder that there will come a point where it is too late. Being who you want to be, and doing what you want to do, does have a very real expiry date. When the thought of running out of time becomes louder than the fear of failure, it does become much easier to step outside your comfort zone, put yourself out there, and become more visible.

Death is as much a part of life as birth. There is nothing wrong with thinking about it well before it happens. I recommend you do. As Socrates, the ancient Greek philosopher, said: *Death may be the greatest of all human blessings.* Do not fear the end; fear not living your life to the fullest.

My music choices for my funeral may change, and new faces may appear in my vision, but I know for sure the day will come. I pray that by then I will be able to pass on surrounded by love and with no regrets at all. I hope the same applies to you. Surely, that is worth thinking about every day. What do you want your loved ones to say about you at your funeral?

If Vanessa's letter touched you, and you would like to help raise money in her name, feel free to donate at - www.garvan.org.au/white-butterfly

BODY

You have one face and one body.
Make the most of it on the path to putting
yourself out there and living a bigger life.

Here are some practical ways to
help you do that.

Make Mindset Part of your Beauty Routine

Wrinkles should merely indicate where smiles have been.

Mark Twain, *writer and humourist*

I had sunk to my lowest of lows. I had been feeling flat for a few months. It felt as though I had hit my emotional rock bottom. Nothing obvious or dramatic triggered the downward spiral; it was a combination of unmet expectations, several missed opportunities work-wise, and a sudden realisation that I was ageing like the best of us.

Aside from feeling physically low and emotionally out of sorts, every time I looked in the mirror, I hated what I saw. I stared into eyes of pure anger, tinged with regret, shame, hurt, sadness and pain. This toxic mix of feelings was the direct result of the ugly thoughts looping inside my head.

Have you ever heard the expression: *It's written all over your face*? I would like to suggest that ugly thoughts create an ugly face. No amount of expensive designer face cream, Botox, or whatever else is available will hide thoughts of self-loathing, shame and anger (to name a few). My thoughts were the ugliest they had been for a very long time. The mirror did not lie.

Having dedicated much of my adult life to self-study, even in my lowest moments I was aware of everything I was thinking and how it was impacting me on all levels of my being. During the few weeks I spent battling with my demons and looking worse for wear, there were 5 distinct and horrid thoughts circling in my mind repetitively. Here they are in black and white:

I am nothing

I am worthless

I am ugly

I am old

I ruin everything

These destructive thoughts had a direct impact on my appearance. The usual sparkle in my eyes was no longer there; my face was grey, the corners of my lips dipped down, the frown lines on my forehead became prominent, and everything seemed to droop. Even my husband commented afterward that the gloomy energy made me look like a different person.

Several heartfelt pep talks, inspirational reading, prayer, meditation, yoga, and time spent in nature (not to mention a haircut, manicure, pedicure and a little shopping) brought me back to light. I am no Robinson Crusoe; we all journey through ups and downs. On this recent trip to the dark side, I realised that my deep dive into this sickening swirl of unhelpful thoughts and emotions had many gifts to offer. Wisdom, compassion, empathy and gratitude are a few of the souvenirs I returned with.

We live in a society obsessed with appearances, spending billions of dollars attempting to create the holy grail of youth. I am not afraid to accept my vanity, and there is nothing wrong with wanting to look our very best at all times. As they say, when we look our best, we feel our best. So, it goes without saying that looking our best helps us play a better game.

If you want to look your best, you have to think your best. If you want to look beautiful, think beautiful thoughts. Your mindset is the most essential part of your beauty and grooming routine; without inner beauty, there can be no external beauty.

The first step is becoming aware of what your thoughts are and accepting you have the power to change them and or let them go. Stop, listen, focus and reflect. What thoughts come to mind when you look in the mirror?

> *If you are genuinely dedicated to looking your best, you need to think your best.*

The benchmark for looking and feeling your best should be your personal best, not an airbrushed illusion of perfection. If you get caught up in beauty trends, be prepared to go on a self-esteem rollercoaster ride. I came across a quote on social media that perfectly makes the point: *Beauty trends are forever changing. Being size zero was once in. People mocked big lips. Curly perm was in, then straightening. I remember when boob jobs were the thing to do. Now lots of women are taking out their implants. Mainstream media mocked big butts. Now lots of people are getting surgery for them. If our self-esteem is connected to 'trends', we will never be content with ourselves.*

Imagine if every morning, as part of your beauty routine, after showering, putting on your facial products and doing your hair, you intentionally took a few minutes to direct your thoughts to self-love and gratitude.

If beautiful thoughts lead us to looking and feeling our best, surely it is worth our time and attention. Once it becomes a habit and you experience the energetic benefits of thinking loving thoughts, looking good will only be the cherry on the big, beautiful, delicious cake of your life!

Always Wear Red Lipstick (Metaphorically Speaking)

A flower does not think of competing with the flower next to it. It just blooms.

Ogui, Japanese sensei, Zen Shin Talks

I represented a supermodel for almost a decade and learned a thing or two about the destructive impact of comparing yourself unfavourably to others. Being up close and personal with one of the most beautiful women in the world, I would constantly measure myself against everything I thought she had and I lacked.

Looking back, I realise how much of my client's life and career I would not choose. But at the time, I had stars in my eyes and a very distorted perspective of myself. Everything changed the moment I began to appreciate my ability to stand out and, believe it or not, this story centres around red lipstick.

I hosted a breakfast event for my client in a stunning private waterfront home in one of Sydney's most exclusive suburbs. All of Australia's leading beauty editors were invited to attend. We had a guest chef from LA cooking up a deliciously healthy menu, cold-pressed juices on tap, and an endless array of beauty products to play with. If it sounds glamorous, I promise it was.

I dealt with feeling small in the presence of my client by focusing on being smart. I thought that if I was never going to match her level of physical beauty and presence, I would focus on looking, acting and appearing intelligent. Embarrassing to admit it now, but I wanted to project an image of being too 'smart' to worry about what I looked like and was content on this occasion to remain physically invisible.

As I stood at the door checking off arrivals and doing my best to keep the event running to plan, I felt a hand tightly grab the back of my arm. I swung round to see a close friend, a well-known beauty executive, only inches from my face. Before I had a chance to say anything she said, "For God's sake, go up and put on some red lipstick. I can see what you are doing, and it's time to stop playing so small." I was speechless.

I felt her every word on a cellular level. My friend had seen me, really seen me, and recognised the game I was playing. It was one of those moments in life that seemed so insignificant on the surface, but energetically it was monumental. She was right, it was time I had the *courage to be* seen and stand proudly in my own space. I immediately went upstairs and put on some red lipstick.

Months later, I hosted another event for my client. It was Valentine's Day. We were celebrating the launch of a new product. This time I wore a beautiful red lace dress and bright red lipstick. I couldn't hide even if I tried to.

As I worked my way through the crowded space, weaving around photographers and Sydney's 'it' crowd, I could see my friend smiling in the corner. I walked up to her and smiled back. "I'm wearing my red lipstick," I said. She gave me a big hug, and we both knew there was nothing else to say.

Red lipstick might not be your thing, but what it represents here is the decision to take up your rightful space, to do whatever you can to look and feel your best. Yes, we are all more than what we look like, but there is no denying our appearance can make a difference to how others perceive and interact with us.

Buy the outfit that makes you feel amazing, invest in a great hairstyle, make the effort to groom yourself because you want to look and feel your best. It has nothing to do with measuring yourself against other people, and everything to do with having the courage to be seen, heard and admired.

Once you make the decision to claim your rightful space and let others see you, I promise your approach to style and appearance will change. A new level of self-confidence will inspire different decisions and actions all aimed at making sure people take notice because, as they say, **you're worth it**. What is your version of red lipstick?

Be the First to Smile

*Use your smile to change the world;
don't let the world change your smile.*

Chinese proverb

I grew up with a mum who would go out of her way to smile and say hello to everyone she walked past. It was not unusual for us to be out on a walk and suddenly stand still while she happily listened to the life story of an elderly person, the antics of a playful toddler, or just someone craving human connection. Her smile sent a message to the other person that she cared and was open to connecting.

As a teenager, I would groan and moan about having to wait, but now I am older, I see this genuine interest in others as one of Mum's greatest superpowers. She makes the world a better place, and it all starts with her smile.

It seems so small and simple, yet the impact of a smile is far-reaching. A genuine smile can make us look more attractive, live longer, and feel less stressed. The benefits of a real smile are also contagious. Studies have shown that when we smile at other people, they can't help but smile back (unless they try not to). Which means when you smile, you are inspiring others to do the same.

With every reason to smile, it will shock you how little we do smile as adults. The average child smiles 400 times a day, yet for an average adult that number drops to 20 times a day. This figure is heartbreaking to me. Hockey player, Tom Wilson, was quoted as saying: *A smile is happiness you will find right under your nose.* This is a happy truth that many of us go through life failing to recognise.

Smiling also contributes to positively shaping our brand. Research undertaken by the University of Essex shows that smiling makes our face more memorable. We appear to be more trustworthy and more confident. Very good attributes to be known and remembered for.

It is worth considering, however, that context is important. Smiling at a funeral, for example, will make you memorable for all the wrong reasons. I have also had clients admit that they smile when they get nervous, making it hard for them to send the right signal in high-pressure situations. Like any habit, smiling when we're nervous can be dealt with. I suggest you breathe more, slow everything down and explore what techniques will help you relax. Remember, in this instance it's your nerves that are the problem, not your smile.

Most people don't need to be reminded of the importance of context, but they do need to be reminded to make a conscious effort to smile. When I started focusing on my own smiling habits, I intentionally changed this downward trend. Call me vain but knowing it would make me appear younger and more attractive was enough to keep me motivated!

The fact that I could reap these benefits and also benefit everyone around me was too good a deal not to accept.

They say the world smiles back when you smile, and I believe it. It can be a superpower on the path to putting yourself out there and living a bigger life. Create more positive energy by sending more of it out into the world in the form of a smile.

Awareness is key. Take the time to do your own smile audit and keep in mind that when you smile, the whole world smiles back. Are you smiling right now?

Choose Commitments Over Your Feelings

Never make permanent decisions based on temporary emotions.

Anonymous

We all sat in silence and contemplated what seemed like an extremely profound question for first thing in the morning. It was New Year's Day, and I was about to enjoy a soul-affirming yoga class.

I sat in the studio awaiting enlightened instruction from our handsome Brazilian teacher, Julio. Speaking in an accent only handsome Brazilian men seem to use, Julio posed a question to the class: "What is the connection between feelings and commitments?"

After a while, several students gently called out their thoughts. Julio nodded and went on to say something which blew me away: *There are times when it is more important to choose our commitments over our feelings.*

I cannot speak for the rest of the class, but for me it was a light bulb moment. This observation made so much sense.

I had always thought my emotions were there to help me navigate my way through life. I liked to 'feel' my way through situations, relationships and opportunities. If something made me feel happy, I would do more of whatever it was. If something made me feel scared or angry, I would avoid it like the plague and question my decisions. While this approach may seem reasonable at first glance, what if our relentless pursuit of pleasure and happiness causes us more pain in the long term?

Julio went on to give the example of practising yoga. He explained there would be days we wouldn't 'feel' like practising. However, if we made a commitment, we should aim to honour this, regardless of how we felt. I could immediately see how this was a valuable lesson for all areas of my life, and I made a promise right there and then to honour my new **commitment** to remain **committed** to my **commitments**.

> *I made a promise right there and then, to honour my new commitment, to remain committed to my commitments.*

As I walked out of the studio into the summer heat, I began to question where in my life I let my feelings derail my commitments. I looked back on the career opportunities I did not pursue out of feeling fearful, and the new skills I gave up on too early out of frustration and embarrassment.

Had I not listened to my negative feelings, by now I would be a harpist, fluent in Spanish, able to dance the tango, have a black belt in Wing Chun, and have written more than one book!

Do our commitments change as we change? Absolutely. I am not suggesting we should keep doing something that is making us miserable. However, questioning our emotions allows us to know the difference between negative feelings that lead to growth, versus pain and discomfort that offers no long-term value.

Mark Manson expresses this insight perfectly in his international bestselling book *The Subtle Art of Not Giving a F*ck*: '*Just because something feels good doesn't mean it is good. Just because something feels bad it doesn't mean it is bad. Emotions are merely signposts, suggestions that our neurobiology gives us, not commandments. Therefore, we shouldn't always trust our own emotions. In fact, I believe we should make a habit of questioning them.*'

Should we stop seeking pleasure and happiness? Absolutely not.

Is it healthy to trade short-term pleasure for long-term fulfilment? Absolutely.

On the path to living a bigger life and putting ourselves out there, there will be many times we don't feel like doing the things we know we need to do. We won't feel like embarking on activities and opportunities that are different, because they mostly exist outside our comfort zone. But if we remain **committed** to our **commitments** and understand that it is not ideal to make long-term decisions based on short-term feelings, we will have a greater chance of being, doing and having everything we want. Won't that be a great feeling?

Learn to Recognise the Signs of Growth

Hard now, easy later or easy now, hard later.
The choice is yours.

Anonymous

I retreated into the arms of my husband in a blubbering mess. Worried something serious had taken place, he asked, "My God, honey, what happened?" To which I replied, "I pitched to be on television." You can imagine his confusion.

The story does not end there. The producer said 'yes' and a date for my interview was booked. I was there at the studio at my allotted time and the interview was over in less than 3 minutes. I thanked everyone, had a photo with the presenter, and quickly retreated to my car, where I cried again. It was all so overwhelming. I was way out of my comfort zone.

The fear and the tears were not a sign that I was not ready to do the interview. They were simply a sign that I was stretching, growing and pushing myself. If I had read the signs in the wrong way, I would have quickly shut down the opportunity before it came to fruition.

My fear and tears were simply a sign that I was stretching, growing and pushing myself.

On the path to living a bigger life, putting yourself out there, and having the courage to be visible, you won't always feel comfortable. Chances are, most of the time it will be the exact opposite. Learning to recognise the different kinds of fear in our life is important. Walking down a dark alley and someone suspicious starts following you? Feel the fear and run away. Putting yourself out there and showing up to help attract bigger and better opportunities into your life? Feel the fear and run towards it.

Steven Pressfield, one of my favourite thinkers and author of *The War of Art,* writes: Are you paralysed with fear? That's a good sign. Fear is good. Like self-doubt, fear is an indicator. Fear tells us what we have to do. Remember one rule of thumb: the more scared we are of work or calling, the surer we can be that we have to do it.

As they say, everything you want is on the other side of fear. The problem is most of us assume that if we are scared, it is a sign we shouldn't be doing the thing that's worrying us in the first place. Now, when I feel scared, I know it is more likely to be a sign I **should** do something. Writing this book is a perfect example. I can't tell you how many excuses and self-sabotaging behaviours came into play in an unconscious effort to not face the fear of failure.

One of the reasons we are so bad at reading the signs is because we assume other people around us are not feeling the same fear and hesitation. This is an invaluable insight I have gained while coaching clients. Clients will share with me stories of people, peers and colleagues they admire. They have placed these individuals up on a pedestal and, when asked whether they think that person feels fear, insecurity and lack of confidence, my clients typically respond with a blank stare.

Just contemplating the possibility that the person they admire has the same difficult feelings but is still taking steps towards leading a big life and career, starts to shift their perspective. We all feel the fear, some of us are just better at interpreting the fear and using it to power our efforts rather than paralyse them.

In case you have put your issues down to imposter syndrome, just remember, **real frauds don't suffer from imposter syndrome**. No matter what you look like, what you have achieved, how many degrees and accolades you have accumulated, there will always be a part of you questioning whether you are good enough. Accept this as a sign you are human and not a fraud.

Next time you are scared to do something new, tune in and ask yourself: Is this fear a sign I am on the right track?

Tap into the Charismatic Power of Caring

True charisma comes from a genuine desire to understand and uplift others.

Michelle Obama, *lawyer, writer and former First Lady of the US*

I have always admired the way some people are able to walk into a room and immediately capture everyone's attention. There is something about them that is unapologetically magnetic. They light up the space they are in and exude an undeniable, energetic presence. Well, now I know their secret.

The word that describes it perfectly is 'charisma'. According to the Oxford Dictionary, charisma is a *compelling charm that can inspire devotion in others.* In an article published in *Psychology Today*, charisma was described as *an energetic spark – something intangible and hard to pinpoint that magnetises you to someone.*

Most people believe charisma is something you either have, or you don't. They have bought into the idea that charisma is a gift from the gods bestowed only on those destined to be prominent figures, famous personalities and confident extroverts. Most people are wrong.

Charisma is a way of being and a set of actions that can be developed in anyone, anywhere. Being charismatic is a decision and the real magic starts when you stop thinking about yourself.

In the words of Michelle Obama: *True charisma comes from a genuine desire to understand and uplift others.* Charisma isn't therefore about **being** captivating; it's about making others feel you are captivated by **them**. When I discovered charisma was less to do with me, and more to do with the focus and care I energetically directed towards others, the path to becoming charismatic became less intimidating.

> *Being charismatic is a decision*
> *and the real magic starts when you*
> *stop thinking about yourself.*

If you were to research all the ways to embody charisma, you would come across tips such as make better eye contact, smile more, nod your head to show you are listening, lean in when talking to others, make sure your body is facing the right direction, and a myriad of other strategies. But there is another way that is quite frankly more powerful and intuitive. Put simply: find a reason to care.

When you care about another person or group of people, your body sends all the right signals automatically; you naturally exude charisma. You are genuinely interested in who they are, and you listen attentively. You remain present to their company. You exhibit warmth. You act compassionately. You take the time to understand them. These are all qualities that create an aura of charisma. So, it pays to find a reason to care about the people you are connecting with from the get-go.

In *The Charisma Myth*, author Olivia Fox Cabane shares a tip from a colleague who, when speaking to another person, visualises them with angel wings. This offers a heartfelt reminder of the inherent worth and essence of every individual. It allows her colleague, who happens to be a neuroscientist, to look past any surface level differences or preconceived biases and remain present. How could you not pay attention and care when speaking to an angel?

I have heard it said that *everyone is someone's somebody*. Whether it is visualising a person you meet with angel wings or reminding yourself the person in front of you is someone's mum, dad, grandparent, son, daughter or friend, there is always a reason to care. We might look different, come from different places, believe in different things, and even live differently; but at our core we are all just trying our best to live, learn and love.

There is an important catch to this insight. You can't pretend to care. Even though charisma is less about who you are and more about what you do, if your actions come from a place that is not genuine, everything you do will end up feeling fake. Our bodies don't lie. In the words of Allen

Ruddock, Irish martial arts teacher and writer: *"Your body communicates as well as your mouth. Don't contradict yourself."*

Your body will reflect your true feelings, whether you want it to or not. Real care leads to being charismatic. Fake care leads to being a phoney.

If it is a matter of listening to your head or your heart, I promise that, in this case, the heart wins. What will it take for you to care more about the people around you?

Unlock Confidence by Changing Your Pose

Our bodies change our minds, our minds can change our behavior, and our behavior can change our outcomes.

Dr Amy Cuddy, *psychologist and author*

His arms looked like they were superglued to his torso. I was in a coaching session with a client we will call Luke, and I pointed out that he always looked rigid in the upper half of his body. Luke admitted it was a force of habit due to nervousness. I suggested that his body language was making him feel even more nervous!

Feeling relaxed and confident is almost impossible when our body is reinforcing negative thoughts and feelings. Without being consciously aware of it, our body posture can make us look, feel and act small.

> *Without being consciously aware of it, our body posture can make us look, feel and act small.*

In her powerful book, *Presence*, Dr Amy Cuddy demonstrates that not only does our thinking affect our body language, but the reverse is also true. Our body language can have a dramatic impact on our thinking. As a psychologist who was teaching leadership at Harvard University at the time of writing her book, Cuddy shares details of a research study that explores how expansive power postures can lead to expansive, powerful thoughts and feelings: The way you carry yourself is a source of personal power – the kind of power that is the key to presence. It's the key that allows you to unlock yourself – your abilities, your creativity, your courage, and even your generosity.

I agree with Cuddy. The way we carry ourselves is a source of personal power. In the moments you do feel small, the simple act of standing bigger will make a difference. By doing so, you will change the way others see you and, more importantly, you will send a silent message to yourself that you are here for a reason, that you deserve to be seen, heard and valued.

Luke made a conscious effort to change. He purposely relaxed his arms before a meeting and intentionally spread out his body during the meeting. The results were immediate. Luke reported back, saying his new body language made him feel and act like a completely different person. He felt more relaxed and confident, which had a positive ripple effect on how he showed up and connected with others. One small shift in his body language created a huge pivot in his mind, body and brand. I know this to be true in my own life and career.

> *One small shift in his body
> language created a huge pivot
> in his mind, body and brand.*

If you ever attend an event where I am speaking, chances are you will find me in a toilet cubicle, standing in a power pose for 2 minutes, while saying a prayer before I go on stage. Call me crazy, but this ritual helps me get into a state of poise and presence.

By standing in a power pose prior to going on stage, I am giving my inner self permission to step into my power and shine. You can do the same. By changing your pose, especially in high stakes moments, you can unlock confidence when you need it most.

What is your body saying about you right now?

In case it is helpful, here is the prayer I use before I go on stage:

> *Dear God, Angels, Ancestors Past and Present,
> Please help me be who I need to be.
> Please help me say what I need to say.
> Please help me show up in a way that allows each
> and every person I will speak to today to discover
> the magic and beauty within them.
> Thank you for allowing me to be a
> channel of light and love.
> Thank you.*

Embody the Magic of Serendipity

Opportunity dances with those already on the dance floor.

H Jackson Brown Jr, *author*

The places you go, the rooms you find yourself in, and the people you meet along the way play a big part in shaping the opportunities you attract and the life you create. It all starts with making sure you are in the right room. Literally.

My life was transformed after relocating to a health retreat in my early 20s. My career in PR can be traced back to attending one seminar, and I married the man of my dreams after we reconnected at a business networking event. In all instances, my physical presence in the right place at the right time changed the course of my destiny.

My physical presence in the right place at the right time changed the course of my destiny.

Steven Pressfield sent a clear message to the world when he wrote *Put Your Ass Where Your Heart Wants to Be*. In this book he writes: Tremendous power lies in the simple, physical act of stationing our body at the epicentre of our dream. There is magic in putting our ass where our heart wants to be. I agree entirely.

Our body is the vessel we have in this lifetime to help us be, do and have all the things we want and dream of. It is the conduit between the dreams we have, and our ability to manifest them in the physical world. I live by the words of French priest and scientist, Pierre Teilhard de Chardin, who said: *We are not human beings having a spiritual experience; we are spiritual beings having a human experience.* Your body is the vehicle you have to journey through this lifetime. I find this idea liberating and exhilarating.

> *Our body is the conduit between the dreams we have and our ability to manifest them in the physical world.*

For the introverts hoping to change the world from the comfort of your home office and computer, I am sorry to say that **putting yourself out there** also refers to your physical body. As energetic and social creatures, no amount of virtual interaction can replace the power and benefits of in-person connection.

This is why it is important we put our bodies in the place where possibility resides. In doing so we open ourselves up to **engineered serendipity**. This is the idea of planning (engineered) the unplanned (serendipity). How is this even possible? First, you must be out there to meet with opportunity. Let me give you a sparkling example.

> *As energetic and social creatures,*
> *no amount of virtual interaction*
> *can replace the power and benefits*
> *of in-person connection.*

I have always kept and created vision boards, or, more, accurately vision books. *Psychology Today* describes a vision board as *a collage of images that represent goals and dreams.* My vision books are filled with cut-out images of the futures I have dreamt of. The contents of my vision books have changed as much as I have over time.

In my 20s, my vision book was filled with images of travel, romance, career, and believe it or not, diamonds. As a romantic Piscean, diamonds have always been a symbol of love, which is why the vision book at the centre of my story had pages filled with images of diamond rings, earrings and necklaces.

Ideally, you are meant to look at your vision board/book daily. However, because of an international move, my vision book was packed away and it would be sometime between sightings. As you will soon discover, that didn't lessen its magical influence. I'm happy to say, this story involves lots of diamonds!

He had my attention when he said he worked in the diamond industry. By later saying his family had one of the largest collections of pink diamonds in the world, he had me enraptured. I was at an industry event for women and sitting next to a gentleman whose family business was one of the official sponsors. His name was Michael Neuman, and he was a qualified gemmologist for Mondial Pink Diamond Atelier. It was a last-minute decision for me to attend the event, and I found myself absolutely delighted by this chance encounter.

What started as a friendly conversation at that event would grow over the years into a professional engagement. I would go on to represent Mondial and partner with their Creative Director, Nadia Neuman, to help launch Australia's first ever Marriage Equality ring. The campaign was a huge success, and we were able to enrol global superstars to be photographed wearing the ring, including the likes of Elton John, Deepak Chopra and Paula Abdul, alongside a long list of local Australian celebrities.

I was also lucky enough to have the privilege of borrowing and wearing Mondial's diamond collection whenever I had any special events to attend. It was like having my own personal jewellery box that doubled as an exclusive boutique. It was a joyful experience, but what makes it unforgettable was the moment I learned there was magic involved.

Years later, while unpacking several old boxes, I stumbled across my old vision book. Excited to revisit my dreams, I looked at one of the pages and gasped out loud. There it was, a cut-out picture of an award-winning piece, designed by none other than Nadia Neuman from Mondial. This image had been glued into one of the pages of my dream book years before the brand and family played such a special role in my life. Call it a coincidence, if you like. I prefer to call it engineered serendipity.

Had I not attended the event that day, I would have missed out on a remarkable chapter of my life, and one I clearly wished for.

I may not have ended up calling the necklace my own, but I got something even more priceless. I was offered proof that dreams do come true in the most unusual ways when you put yourself out there. So, trust the process, and get out onto the dance floor of opportunity. Where are you going this week, month, year?

Act Your Spirit, Not Your Age

*I don't know how to act my age.
I've never been this age before.*

Skylar Blue, *multifaceted entertainer*

At the young age of 55, my mum sold her apartment, gave away most of her belongings, packed up the rest and went on a solo adventure around the world.

She went trekking through Spain, paragliding in Croatia, hot air ballooning in Turkey and detoxed in the lush rainforests of Thailand. During her travels she met a man, fell deeply in love, and decided to relocate from Sydney to Barcelona permanently. Together they launched a travel business called Crossroads Travel, helping others walk the Camino De Santiago, the ancient pilgrimage believed to help visitors connect and discover the deeper meaning to life. Mum is my hero.

Act your spirit, not your age.

Through her actions, she showed me it is never too late to start again. It is never too late to set off on an adventure and put your faith in what life has to offer. While some people might see their 50s as the runway to retirement, my mum went running towards the unknown. She was acting her spirit, not her age, and I hope I am brave enough to do the same as I get older.

There is no denying age does change things, but research shows that even on a physical level, our mindset can have a dramatic impact on the extent to which we do age.

In the 1970s, a famous experiment conducted by Harvard psychologist Ellen Langer and her team set out to measure whether thinking young would result in acting young. A group of elderly participants were invited to a 1-week retreat to relive their past, literally. The retreat had been retrofitted to look and feel like the past. Everything had been recreated to make them feel as if they had travelled back in time and were back in the 50s. The results were astonishing.

Langer reported that many participants showed improvements in physical strength, manual dexterity, gait, posture, perception, memory, cognition, taste sensitivity, hearing and vision. Proof to me that even something as physical as ageing is impacted by attitude, perception and intention.

I know people who have proven to me that ageing is inevitable, but growing old is a choice. Take my mentor as the perfect example.

Leon is in his 70s. He brags about his ability to do chin-ups, dresses like he is in his 20s (in a good way) and is full of energy. I have never seen or felt Leon's age and I know that is intentional. He doesn't act his age, nor does he talk about it. Even after a serious surgery that could have cost him his life, I did not hear Leon complain once. Nothing seems to dampen his larger-than-life presence and positive attitude. I want to be like Leon when I grow up.

Making excuses about one's age applies to both ends of the spectrum. Once you are a fully developed adult, there is also no such thing as being too young to do something. If you take the time to look, you will find individuals who are brave enough to go against the conventions of age and choose the rules for how their life should unfold, regardless of the stage they are at.

You are where you are, whether you like it or not. You can't turn back the hands of time, and God only knows why anyone would ever want to speed it up. Be grounded in where you are at and make your own rules about how you want to be at your age. In the words of my idol, Iris Apfel, who recently passed away at the young age of 103: *What's wrong with being 72 or 82 or 92? If God is good enough to give you those years, flaunt them.* As a magazine cover girl aged 100, Apfel did just that.

If you feel like you are stuck in an age rut, make the effort to find new friends that are younger and older, so you have a diversity of thought, experience and insight in your life.

When you spend time with people who are older, you realise how young you are and, in my experience, spending time with people who are younger, makes you feel younger. It is a win all round.

Next time you hear yourself say, 'I am too old,' or 'I am too young,' ask yourself: Are you acting your spirit or your age?

Reinvent Yourself from the Outside In

Every morning, we get a chance to be different. A chance to change. A chance to be better. Your past is your past. Leave it there. Get on with the future part, honey.

Nicole Williams, *Lost & Found*

I clearly remember this woman walking into the hairdressing salon where I was working, on a mission.

I had just been given freedom to take on my own clients, which meant new clients to the salon were automatically allocated to me. As she sat in front of me, in no time at all I would discover this client had just been through a messy divorce and wanted to completely reinvent herself. I willingly and, if I am honest, nervously, obliged.

As her hair fell to the ground, it felt as if she was letting go of whole aspects of her past as well.

Over the course of 3 hours and several glasses of champagne, she went from having a long blonde conservative hairstyle to a short, bright red, utterly vivacious bob. The transformation was dramatic, and the results were immediate. It wasn't so much the hair I remember; it was her entire demeanour. In that moment, she was giving herself permission to change from the outside in.

What I witnessed that day was the power of reinventing yourself. When it comes to creating personal change, starting on the surface is sometimes the best place to begin. One thing is for sure, no one will ever be able to convince me that we are unable to change. If anyone tells you *a leopard never changes its spots*, just remind them we are human and can always go to the hairdresser.

> *If anyone tells you a leopard never changes its spots, just remind them we are human and can always go to the hairdresser.*

It is undeniable that what we wear and how we present ourselves does have an impact on how we feel, the way we think, and how others perceive us. One of my closest friends, award-winning journalist and bestselling author, Kathryn Eisman, has dedicated most of her adult life to decoding the psychology of style. She launched an international television series *Undressed with Kathryn Eisman* that explores how changing our clothes can change our lives. The series follows the stories of everyday individuals who were willing to put the theory to the test. The aim was to change their lives by changing their clothes. I promise that, after watching it, you will never look at your wardrobe the same way again.

In the first episode, Kathryn says, "Science shows that brains love routine; we eat the same breakfast, wake up at the same time and the same is true when it comes to getting dressed." She continues, "It's called Repetitious Wardrobe Complex: wearing the same thing over and over again. You have to look at the outcome. Are you feeling the way you want to feel? Are you getting the results and feedback you want from the world? If the answer is 'no', what do you need to do? Change your clothes."

> *What we wear and how we present ourselves does have an impact on how we feel, the way we think, and how others perceive us.*

There are times when change starts from the inside, and the way we present ourselves on the outside no longer feels aligned. In those instances, remaining open to new possibilities is what matters. It starts with giving ourselves permission to embody the new version of ourselves that is emerging. This is a vital lesson I was reminded of through a wonderful client of mine. For the purpose of this story, I will call her Christine.

Christine hobbled towards me with a moon boot on. I was meeting her for the first time. She had injured her leg and decided to use the downtime to reinvent herself.

We sat down, and I was as nervous as she was. Christine was nervous because she found the idea of putting herself out there daunting. I was nervous because she was one of my first ever coaching clients (I was still working out exactly what to do as a personal brand coach). As it turned out, we were made for each other.

We discussed her vision for a book, her desire to get out on the speaking circuit, and her drive to create a personal brand. We spoke at length, worked on new ideas and mapped out some of the things she would need to consider. All in all, the suggested changes we came up with meant reinventing her personal brand and trusting the vision of her future self.

The transformation was remarkable.

As Christine wrote the book she'd been longing to write, a new person began to emerge. With every chapter, she allowed more of her future self to come to the fore. She lost half her body weight and with that gained the confidence to elevate her style. This transformation did not happen accidentally. She gave herself permission to change and had the courage to wear it out loud.

When I was growing up, my dad would often say to me, *"Life is not a dress rehearsal."* The older I get, the more I appreciate that sentiment. We really do only get one chance to dress up and be the character we want to play in this lifetime.

One quick test to determine whether who you are on the outside is reflecting who you want to be on the inside, is to look in the mirror. Look at yourself. Do you connect with what you see? Do you feel it is time to change? Are you stuck in the past? Are you suffering from Repetitious Wardrobe Complex in a bad way? Only you know the answers, and only you hold the key to your transformation.

As they say: *You are always one decision away from a totally different life.* Maybe that decision is staring you in the face. Is it time to reinvent yourself?

BRAND

You have the power to decide who you are, what you stand for, and how to present yourself to the world.

It all starts with having the *courage to be* the brand in you.

Create a Personal Brand with Purpose

Service to others is the rent you pay for your time here on earth.

Muhammad Ali, *professional boxer and activist*

For most of my career, I didn't think my personal brand mattered.

I wasn't a celebrity, CEO or public figure. I could understand why it was important for my clients to shape their personal brand, but I could not see how it was relevant to me. I fooled myself into thinking there was some sort of imaginary level I had to reach to consider myself important enough to worry about my personal brand.

I am here to tell you that there is no level, and your personal brand does matter. Taking control of who you are, what you stand for, and how you communicate your value to the world is a form of personal power. It gives you the ability to attract the things you want, and the confidence to know what opportunities to chase. Whether you are visible to one person or many, you are in control of what they see, hear and experience.

Nothing about personal branding is accidental. If you spend any time researching the topic of personal branding, however, you will inevitably come across someone saying: We all have a personal brand, whether we shape it or not. I disagree entirely.

A personal brand is the intentional way an individual presents and packages themselves for a **purpose**. To suggest we have a personal brand without consciously shaping one would be like saying a busy street food vendor in Bangkok is as much of a 'brand' as McDonald's. While both might have a reputation for serving a particular type of fast food, one clearly is a brand and the other is not. One is consistent, cohesive and clearly communicates what it has to offer, whereas the other doesn't.

The act of personal branding is deliberate. A clearly defined brand allows you to communicate your point of difference, values and purpose clearly. It enables you to harness the power of visibility, create a loyal following and, as I mentioned before, attract the right kinds of opportunities.

When done for the right reasons, with a focus on **intention** rather than **attention**, a personal brand can offer you a powerful platform to impact the lives of those around you positively. Though the term 'personal brand' suggests it is all about you, the benefits of creating a personal brand can be far-reaching when it is centred around serving others.

Aiming to serve and embracing our ability to uplift, inspire, educate and inform can change the game. In the words of motivational great, Jim Rohn: *"Service to others leads to greatness."* It is about using our self, image and likeness as a vehicle for the greater good, rather than feeding our ego. It all starts with reflecting on your **purpose** and then considering your 4Ps.

I spent my 20s preoccupied with 'finding' my purpose. I looked for it in people, places, retreats, workshops and experiences. I was forever waiting for the magical moment where I would simply know what I was meant to do and why. I eventually gave up trying to 'find' my purpose when I realised there was a much better solution. Purpose isn't something you find; it is something you choose.

> *Purpose isn't something you find;*
> *it is something you choose.*

If you are struggling to articulate or choose your purpose, I highly recommend you do some research into the powerful Japanese concept called *ikigai*, loosely translated to mean 'reason for living'.

To discover your ikigai, you need to ask yourself the following 4 questions:

- What am I good at?
- What do I love to do?
- What can I be paid for?
- What problem am I solving, and for whom?

At the intersection of your answers, you will find some insightful clues into who you are and your unique point of difference. I suggest my clients use the same 4 questions to find their personal brand X factor.

The 4Ps of Personal Branding

Once you have established clarity surrounding your purpose, it is time to consider your 4Ps:

1. Promise

2. Packaging

3. Position

4. Promotion

Whenever I present the 4Ps of personal branding to an audience, I help bring the material to life by using the analogy of a well-known product and brand. Most of the time, it is a Rolex watch.

We all intuitively understand the purpose and power of the Rolex brand (as well as other topline brands, such as Apple and Coca-Cola), but rarely do we take the time to think about our power and purpose, our own personal brand.

Obviously, there is an important distinction to make between our personal brand and the big product brands out there. The

Rolex is not human. As humans, we are multi-dimensional, ever evolving, creative beings. The Rolex has been designed for a particular purpose, with a specific audience in mind. It is inanimate and can remain the same for a long period of time. We can't.

To think you will ever create a personal brand that will remain static is futile. You will change, as will your brand. But never forget, you control the narrative every step of the way. Let's give it a go now, starting with your promise.

Promise

Thinking about a Rolex watch, we can easily sum up its promise in 2 words: time and status. A functional Rolex watch delivers on its promise every time an individual uses it. Not only can it be relied on to tell the time accurately, but there is a level of status that goes into making the wearer feel special.

When thinking about what your promise might be, we want to approach it from 2 different angles. First, what is your **Intellectual Promise** i.e. What do you want others to think about when they think of you? What do you do? Then, there is your **Energetic Promise** i.e. How do you want others to consistently feel when in your company? Let me explain.

Your **Intellectual Promise** can be summed up by the things you do and want to be known for, such as your areas of expertise and skills. When someone thinks of your name, what words, phrases or ideas do you want them to automatically think of? For me, my Intellectual Promise can be summed up in words and phrases, such as personal branding, influence and international speaker.

One question that might help you articulate your Intellectual Promise is this: What kind of opportunities would you like to attract more of?

Your **Energetic Promise** is how you want others to feel in your presence. Emotions are contagious. We have all experienced how contagious emotions can be and research can confirm this. When you recognise you are having a 'bad day', there is a very good chance you are unintentionally creating the same reality for everyone around you.

From a personal branding perspective, becoming intentional about your **Energetic Promise** and the emotional ripples you create, starts with considering how to relate to others in a way that's consistent. This approach doesn't just apply to in-person interactions; research has shown that online emotions expressed in your posts on social media are equally contagious.

Some of the words included in my Energetic Promise are: uplifting, empowering, confident, safe, calm and caring. I try to ensure my presence, actions and points of communication always resonate with my promise.

Having a clear Energetic Promise will help you be intentional about the impact you want to have on the people around you, and decisive on how to make that happen.

In an interview conducted for Stanford University Graduate School, Leena Nair, Global CEO of Chanel, shared that **compassion** is a guiding principle for her. She went on to suggest that during meetings she makes a point of ensuring everyone around the table has an opportunity to speak. She defines compassion as 'having an understanding for people'. Compassion is part of Nair's Energetic Promise. In her own words, "For me, it really matters that I set a brand of leadership that is about compassion, empathy. Do the tough things, do it decisively, but do it with compassion, keeping the human being at the end of it, who is impacted by your decisions, in mind."

Think about how you want to make others feel? When making others feel good about themselves becomes part of your personal brand, it is an emotional win-win for everyone.

Feel free to write your thoughts in the section below:

My Intellectual Promise is:

....
....
....
....

My Energetic Promise is:

....

....

....

....

Packaging

If I were to hand you a Rolex watch in a dirty plastic bag, there is a good chance you would assume I was gifting you a fake timepiece. It would dramatically change the impression and experience you have of the watch.

Brands spend millions of dollars creating the perfect packaging for this exact reason. They know that how the product is packaged will have a substantial impact on the way it is perceived.

The same applies to us as individuals. When considering how you package yourself, it is important to consider all the ways others interact with you. In person and online are 2 obvious places to start.

In person, we need to consider your image, grooming, personal style and body language. Are you intentional about the way you carry yourself? Do you carefully consider your body language? What does your personal style say about you? Is your style sending and reinforcing the message you want it to?

Everything you do and don't do; everything you wear and don't wear; the brands you use and don't use, all go into shaping the picture the world sees of who you are and what you stand for. Whether you like to accept it or not, when you meet another person or group of people, within as little as a tenth of a second, they have scanned you and created a first impression of who they think you are.

While you cannot completely control and manage what other people think of you, there are certainly powerful ways for you to influence it.

I remember having a conversation with a prominent medical director in London. He had been invited to interview for a high-profile position at a very exclusive private hospital. To prepare for the meeting he went out and invested in a new designer suit, a smart looking pen, and immaculately clean shoes. He was intentional in the way he presented himself, because he knew it would, and does, make a difference.

I have seen firsthand the transformative change that occurs when clients change their style. They end up looking different. They also feel and act differently, with more purpose and presence. Whether it is wanting to look and feel more powerful or breaking the mould of an outdated style that is ageing them unnecessarily, there is something so exciting about watching a person have fun and being willing to experiment with this area of their brand.

However, style is only one part of the bigger picture. It is not just what you wear, it is also about how you use your body, your voice, your choice of words and the actions you take. If this feels complicated, I agree it is. Yet when you are clear on your intentions, I assure you that the ripple effect you create is automatic. You become clearer about what feels right and wrong, on brand and not.

If you are confused about what your intentions are or should be, start to think about what you admire in others. What traits, characteristics, style decisions and actions do you aspire to embody in your life and in your way of operating? It is not about copying or trying to be like someone else entirely, it is about consciously deciding who will influence you and why. That applies to the physical world, as well as the digital world.

In an interview with Tim Ferris, Mark Zuckerberg, founder of Meta, suggested, *"There's a physical world and a digital world. The real world is actually both."* I can't help but agree.

Once you have considered how you want to package yourself in the physical realm, you need to then consider your online self. Are your online profiles consistent with the way you show up offline? If I met you in person and then looked you up online, would I feel like I was meeting the same person or someone completely different? Or would I question why you look 10 years younger on social media? It goes without saying, the aim is for your online and offline self to be one and the same.

On the path to shaping your online self, you will need to think about your profile photography and bio.

Invited to speak or take part in a panel event? The organisers will ask for a profile shot and bio. The media wants to interview you? The journalist will request a profile photo and biographical details. You have been invited to feature on a podcast? The producer will ask you for a profile shot and bio. It is important to get these 2 things right.

Let's start with your profile shot. Research shows that your profile photo can have a dramatic impact on your perceived levels of influence, likeability and credibility. One study, led by researchers at the University of New South Wales (UNSW), also concluded that we are generally bad at choosing flattering photos of ourselves and that we should let other people choose the image we use to put our best face forward.

In an interview with *USA Today*, Dr David White, who led the study said, "The effect of [the profile photo you choose] is likely to have a substantial impact on online interactions, the impressions people form and the decisions they base on them, including whether to employ, date, befriend or even vote for someone. Previous work has shown that people make inferences about an individual's character and personality within a split second of seeing a photograph of their face, so our results have clear practical implications; if you want to put your best face forward, it makes sense to ask someone else to choose your picture."

Take the time to think about what you want your profile image to say, and what message and impression you want to make. Then ask yourself, and those you trust, whether the profile photo you are using is 'on brand' or if it is time to update the shot you've been using.

Next is your bio. An esteemed professor once said to me, *"A bio is more important than a CV,"* and I tend to agree. This is the one document that is designed to powerfully communicate the story of who you are, what you stand for, and why you do what you do. You control the narrative. You decide what achievements, highlights and key messages you want another person to focus on when they think about you and your personal brand.

Just as you would dress to impress, use words to dress up your bio and remember the right choice of words can elevate and enhance. Remember, words and numbers are symbols, and those symbols can carry influence. When writing a professional bio, you ultimately want to use those symbols to harness the flow of influence.

Some things to consider:

- **Commanding and influential adjectives** ~ Think of words such as leading, sought after, celebrated, award-winning (if true), powerful, international, global, cutting edge, and the list goes on and on.

- **Big and impressive numbers** ~ Could be the number of years you have been in the industry to demonstrate your experience or is there another number you might use? A client of mine worked out she had profiled over a 'billion dollars' worth of real estate!

- **Influential people or clients you have worked with** ~ Nothing wrong with a bit of name-dropping. If you have worked with high-profile clients and credible companies, it's a great way to establish credibility and develop personal influence.

If you struggle to write about yourself don't be afraid to use AI platforms to help create a framework you can edit and optimise. Once you have your first draft, read it out loud and see how it makes you feel. Does it resonate? Does the language feel on brand? Will it help you attract the opportunities you are seeking? Does it clearly communicate your purpose and the impact you aim to have?

Your bio, or a version of it, should ideally feature on your social media pages, on your personal website if you have one, the company website if you represent or work for another brand, and be on hand whenever you have an opportunity to promote yourself and the work you do.

Helping others clearly understand who you are and what you offer is a service to them. This applies whether you are trying to reach one person or one million. No one wins if you remain the best kept secret, so don't be afraid to own your story. Package it all up in the most powerful way possible, then share it with others.

Position

When talking about position and keeping the Rolex watch in mind, I ask my audiences, "Would you expect to find a Rolex in the toothpaste aisle of your local supermarket?" I am sure you can guess the answer: No!

Companies, and the brands they represent, understand that where they place their product has an impact on how the customer will experience and perceive that product. The position you find the product in reinforces the intellectual and energetic promise of the product (beauty in the beauty section, watch in the watch section). Placement underlines your energetic promise (affordable or exclusive). And most importantly, make sure you're in a place that makes it easy and obvious to find you (not hidden away where no one can locate you).

Brands also understand the power of association and will go out of their way to make sure the right people are wearing the product. It is essential that the brand is represented at the right events, and any marketing material is featured in the right publications.

The same applies to you as an individual, literally and metaphorically. How you package yourself, where you work, the people you associate with, the things you do, and the places you go, all contribute to the way you're positioned.

The questions are:

- Where and how do you want to be positioned in other people's minds?
- What are you doing to make that happen?

For example, if my Intellectual Promise is personal branding for executives, some of the ways I could position myself is to share relevant social media content, run company workshops, be a panelist at the right kind of industry events, be a guest on career-related podcasts talking about personal branding, maybe even write a book (wink, wink!). It's about turning your ideals into practical action steps and identifying ways to ensure you're placed on the right shelf (metaphorically speaking).

This approach holds true, whether you work for yourself or someone else. For some of the individuals I have had the privilege of coaching, their aim is to be seen, heard, known and positioned well within the company they work for. In that case, things like strategic networking, sharing expertise in a team setting, or running relevant training sessions are some of the tactics they use to position themselves properly.

Sadly, most people leave how they are positioned up to others and, as a result, end up attracting the wrong people, places and opportunities into their life, then are left wondering why. A former client of mine, who I'll call Kelly, is a perfect example.

Kelly was a partner at a high-profile law firm. Her level of experience and expertise meant she was regularly invited by industry and government bodies to contribute her thought leadership. On one occasion, a paper she wrote captured the attention of the media and her ideas began to spread like wildfire. The exposure was incredible, but unfortunately the positioning was wrong.

Kelly wanted to be known for another area of expertise, so we had to take the time to map out an action plan to change her positioning. Some of the considerations that were included in this mix were updating her bio and posting social media content that was more aligned with her chosen area of expertise. Kelly also proactively offered to run a masterclass for a private network of female CEOs, and she pitched several articles to trade media outlets. Kelly took the time to articulate how she wanted to be positioned, then made sure it happened. You can do the same.

> *Most people leave how they are positioned up to others and, as a result, end up attracting the wrong people, places and opportunities into their life and are left wondering why.*

Promotion

Coming back to our Rolex example, we know that getting the product into the exclusive boutique, onto the perfectly manicured shelf, and into the hands of the right ambassadors is not where the story ends. From here, the intentional journey of promoting the product begins. We know that the biggest brands in the world spend the most on promotion, yet often this message gets lost in translation when applied to personal branding.

Most people fall into the trap of thinking, *when I am good enough, then I will be offered the right opportunities to put myself out there and build my profile.* As a former international personal publicist, I know for sure that powerful personal brands are created by individuals who actively seek opportunities to raise their profile. They don't wait for permission or validation. They know if they want an opportunity, they must go out and make it happen. They understand that it is their job to put themselves out there and remain top of mind.

> *They don't wait for permission or validation*
> *They know if they want an opportunity,*
> *they must go out and make it happen.*

I remember, some time ago, sitting down with a veteran journalist who had spent much of his illustrious career writing for the *Australian Financial Review*. He had just started a new career chapter in PR, and we were chatting about personal branding. He confided, "You know, Carlii, in my days we were told to put our head down, butt up, and just work really hard. That was apparently how to get noticed and get ahead."

I quietly nodded, attempting to hide the fact I disagreed with that idea. I didn't have to say anything. He went on to complete his sentence by saying, "What a load of sh*t that was!"

I had to laugh. We both knew the truth. The individuals who ended up being successful were the ones who approached their personal branding professionally. Unless you make a point of getting noticed, your chances of capturing the attention of the right people and building the kind of network that will really elevate you to the top are slim.

I can say, hand on heart, my life changed for the better when I put in the time, effort and resources to shape, manage and elevate my personal brand. I attracted opportunities I never knew were possible. I connected with amazing individuals from all over the world and, most importantly, I felt a real sense of purpose. By becoming clear on what I wanted to represent and who I wanted to serve, I finally tapped into that feeling of purpose I had always been longing for.

We don't serve the world by shrinking and hiding away from view. We serve the world by sharing ourselves, our stories, our skills and our gifts. As they say, create a personal brand for a cause not for applause. Be proud of the value you have to offer and focus on the people you are here to serve. I promise that, on the other side of any fear or hesitation you might be feeling, there is a life and version of yourself you are going to love, and others will be grateful for.

Feel free to visit **www.carliilyon.com/brandidentityguide** for additional resources to help you create a personal brand with a purpose.

Beware of The Thoughts

No one knows what they are doing. You have to put yourself out there and just give it a try.

Reese Witherspoon, *actress and film producer*

Something was simply not right. I could see it in his eyes and in his results. My client was getting to the stage where they were facing The Thoughts. For the purpose of this story, I will call him Nick.

Having travelled around the country speaking about personal branding and consulting to a myriad of incredibly talented individuals, I knew what was coming. Though each of my clients were different, the destructive thoughts were the same.

Our session had come to an end. However, I knew I had to confront Nick. He was about to launch a new venture and proactively start putting himself out there, but he wasn't doing the work. "You know what needs to be done, and quite frankly you could do it in a day, why are you procrastinating?" I gently questioned.

Just as I guessed, he proceeded to share and prove me right. He was having The Thoughts.

It honestly doesn't matter who you are, what you do, how you do it or why you do it, chances are, on the path to putting yourself out there and building your profile, you will inevitably face one or all of the thoughts below, but don't let negative thinking hold you back.

With awareness comes power, the power to decide if you are going to live by these destructive thoughts or simply see them for what they are and let them go. You are the only one who can decide, all I can do is let you know what they are ...

Who am I to speak?

This one belongs at the top of any list of destructive thinking. My suggested response is: Who are you not to speak?! You came into this world with a purpose and something to say. Each one of us can positively influence the lives of others, but all too often we shy away, because we think we don't count and our opinion doesn't matter.

While I accept we are not all here to reach international fame, fortune and influence, we are here to change the world in our own way. Your influence may only stretch to your team or department, but why would you think for a minute that doesn't count. In the words of Buddha: *One moment can change a day, one day can change a life and one life can change the world.*

I am not saying or doing anything new, so why would anyone care?

There is much debate about where thoughts come from, and perhaps we will never truly know. What we do know is original thought is rarely original. We live in a world where we are influenced by all the wonderful things this world has to offer.

As Mark Twain put it: *There is no such thing as a new idea.* He went on to say, "It is impossible. We simply take a lot of old ideas and put them into a sort of mental kaleidoscope. We give them a turn and they make new and curious combinations. We keep on turning and making new combinations indefinitely; but they are the same old pieces of coloured glass that have been in use through all the ages."

However, there is one thing that is unique, and that is you. Whatever you do, you bring your ideas, experiences, stories and gifts to life in your own way, and that is what makes them original!

Everyone will think I have a big ego

The people who accuse you of having a big ego, because you are putting yourself out there and giving something a go, are indeed the same individuals who are completely ruled by their own ego! In fact, these naysayers are so worried about what others will say, they hide away and never positively challenge the status quo.

You need to decide whether their opinions really matter. As they say: *The person you are becoming will cost you people, relationships, spaces and material things.* Choose the person you are becoming over everything.

Thoughts will come and go; it's up to us to decide which thoughts we want to hold onto. According to bestselling author, Byron Katie, *"A thought is harmless, unless we believe it. It is not our thoughts, but the attachment to our thoughts that causes suffering."* So, while these moments of doubt are inevitable, your response to them is your decision alone. Now, that is a thought worth holding onto.

Are one or more of these thoughts holding you back?

Practise Intentional Authenticity

Forgive your younger self. Believe in your current self. Create your future self.

Angeli Marie Shaw, *Holistic Empowerment Coach*

There is a Japanese legend that says we all have 3 faces: the face we show the world; the face we show our close friends and family; and the face we show no one but ourselves. Your personal brand represents the face you show the world. It is how you present, package, and promote yourself in a way that attracts the right people and opportunities into your life.

I am often asked about authenticity and how it fits into personal branding. Well-meaning individuals express their want to show up as their real self but end up confused and questioning which 'self'. Truth is, we are all multi-dimensional. We all have many faces, who we are in one situation, may not be entirely who we are in the next.

For example, who we are at work with peers and colleagues is not necessarily who we are when we are out with our closest friends. That is why asking your friends for advice on your personal branding is not always the best idea. They see and experience a side of you that possibly has nothing to do with the face you want to show the world.

Being intentional about what parts of yourself you want to put on show is no less authentic. In her book *Authentic Gravitas*, Dr Rebecca Newtown puts it this way: Being authentic demands clarity and discipline to sometimes move away from old habits, try new things, and be true to your intention for impact. In short, intentional authenticity is about thinking what kind of impact you want to have and then being true to that.

There are times where **being yourself**, or whatever that represents, is not going to get you to where you want to go. The real power lies in being authentic to who you want to be, rather than who you have always been.

At first, it may feel like you are playing a character, as you try on new habits and behaviours. Sometimes that will mean you have to move through the discomfort of feeling like a fake. I know that is how I felt when I first started putting myself out there. From the outside I looked confident and as if I knew exactly what I was doing. But when I looked in the mirror at the face no one else got to see, I was nervous, unsure and insecure. I had to have the **courage to be**, before I could **become**.

> *I had to have the courage to be,*
> *before I could become.*

There are times where it is healthy and pure to take off the proverbial mask and express your true feelings. Then there are other moments and situations, where putting on a mask may help close the gap between who you are today and who you want to be in the future. This is something I started to seriously explore after coming across the work of Todd Herman.

A high-performance coach and author of *The Alter Ego Effect,* Herman helps his clients, including Olympic athletes, CEOs and high-profile entrepreneurs, unlock their potential by tapping into the power of an alter ego. In the book he writes, "It's incredible how quickly we can change our concepts of what is possible when we adopt a new identity." This thought excited me.

If you google 'celebrities with alter egos', you will find a long list of icons who have used this method to help them rise to the greatest heights of professional success. Superstars including Beyonce, Oprah, Kobe Bryant, Lady Gaga, David Bowie, Bono and Madonna have all called on an alter ego to help them stay true to their intention for impact. Even as seasoned performers, they had to find an effective way to get out of their heads and into being who they wanted to be. If it works for them, surely it can work for us as well.

Some people think this is about being something you are not; I see this as making the effort to be who you want to be.

This is how I've applied the method in my life. I first thought about, then wrote out, the person I wanted to be and how

I wanted others to perceive me. Confident, self-assured, outgoing, intelligent, powerful and well-spoken are some of traits I listed. Some people give their alter ego a name; I didn't, because I saw it as my future self. I then used my red lipstick as the way to switch my alter ego on.

Still to this day, when I put on my red lipstick it marks the moment I transform from being shy and introverted to being on show. I am not pretending; I am simply getting out of my own way so I can stay true to my intention for impact.

> *I am not pretending; I am simply getting out of my own way, so I can stay true to my intention for impact.*

There is another side to being intentionally authentic that is too important not to talk about. That is, being careful not to confuse authenticity with transparency. There is a dangerous idea that suggests being authentic means we must divulge our deepest, darkest secrets and vulnerabilities. It has led individuals to turn their personal struggles into public content, with no real thought given to the long-term consequences.

Please don't get me wrong. I am all about sharing and connecting. I am all for being proud of who you are and representing a message bigger than yourself. At times, sharing a personal story or anecdote is the magic ingredient to making the most impact. What matters is knowing that once you put something out there, it becomes public property.

That is why we need to be intentional about what we share and take the time to be crystal clear on why we are sharing it. How will your story add value to the audience? If it is a challenge or problem you faced, are you coming to the table with a solution? Have you considered the long-term consequences of the things you are sharing?

I remember a conversation I had with a high-profile executive in the corporate world known as the 'fixer'. She is on the speed dial of many influential CEOs and the first person they call in a crisis. In speaking with her about personal branding and leaders putting themselves out there, her word of advice is, "Don't say, do or post anything you wouldn't be happy to have featured on the cover of a newspaper." As a former personal publicist, I completely agree. And that applies to everyone, not just leaders.

Seasoned professionals and experienced public figures know there needs to be a healthy distance between their personal life and their professional life. They accept there is a difference between who they are in their inner world, with their inner circle of friends and family, versus who they are in the world at large. They know that the audience they serve, whether a small team, a company, or millions of followers, are there because they want to be served, informed, led, guided or entertained. Their audience or followers are not the people they will call at 3am in an emergency.

There are parts of myself and my life that are sacred. Too special and important to me to be turned into content for public consumption. The same applies to you. Being intentionally authentic is about unapologetically choosing who you want to be and which parts of yourself you want to put on show. If that's not being real, I'm not sure what is.

Avoid Becoming a Stereotype

The thing about stereotyping is it's usually just throwing rocks into a crowd, hoping to hit somebody who deserves it.

Criss Jami, *author and musician*

I once read a story about a professor who loved speaking to strangers, so much so that while travelling he would go out of his way to make sure he encountered them.

One day he took note of something interesting. Every time he mentioned he was a professor, the person he was speaking to seemed to immediately change. In his words, they would become "respectful, accepting and dull". They assumed that, because he was a professor, they had to show up and act a certain way. As a result, and to avoid any future disappointment, he made a point of not using his title.

This reminds me of a conversation I had with a client who believed she couldn't be herself on social media, because she was trying to attract CEOs. She assumed they would resonate with serious, intelligent and strictly corporate messaging. When I asked her how many CEOs she knew – and she knew a lot! - who were serious, intelligent and strictly corporate at all times, she replied "none".

It is this narrow thinking that leads so many people to play it safe when it comes to their personal branding. Our assumptions about what our audience is like can trip us up. While I understand the convenience of stereotypes, especially when it comes to marketing, the truth is they can be dangerous and misleading.

When we shape our personal brand and cater our messaging to stereotypes, we end up becoming a stereotype. We tend to fade into the noise everyone else is making, all those others also trying to show up as a lawyer, engineer, designer, tech entrepreneur, etc. We tend to look for examples of peers who are 'doing the same thing' because it's safe and predictable. Too often, we are afraid of being the first.

> *When we shape our personal brand and cater our messaging to stereotypes, we also end up becoming a stereotype.*

If you are going to look at others as a measurement for what is right, make sure they are living the life you want to lead. If not, following in their footsteps is not such a wise path to take.

Titles are great, but just remember, behind every title is a flawed human just trying to belong and be accepted for who they are. When you are proud of who you are and show up as yourself, you give others permission to do the same. You also avoid becoming a stereotype or, worse still, feeling like a stereotype.

> *Titles are great, but just remember, behind every title is a flawed human just trying to belong and be accepted for who they are.*

This reminds me of a memorable encounter I had at a women's networking event.

I was invited to be the featured speaker and was there to talk about the power and purpose of personal branding. At the end of the event, a young woman came up to me in tears (not my intended outcome, I assure you).

Worried I had said something to offend her, I asked if she was okay. She let me know they were happy tears and that she found my presentation moving. She asked if she could share her story. Of course, I couldn't wait to hear it.

Turns out, she worked at one of Australia's leading investment banks. She had worked hard to get where she was and loved the work she was doing. Problem was, she was living a double life.

In her own time, away from the stress and serious nature of her office job, she was an aspiring weightlifting and fitness coach. Afraid that her life outside the boundaries of her conservative 9 to 5 office job would destroy her credibility, she did everything she could to hide the truth. In doing so, she felt like she was hiding a big part of who she genuinely wanted to be in the world.

Exhausted by her efforts at keeping up appearances, she decided that being open and living with the consequences would be better than trying to live up to the stereotype. Her first step was updating her LinkedIn profile. That was her way to bring her 2 worlds together. What happened next was remarkable.

Firstly, her clients and colleagues were excited to learn about her expertise in health and wellness. It offered a new path for her to better connect with the people around her and created valuable workplace relationships that went beyond 9 to 5. By updating her LinkedIn profile, she also attracted new coaching clients. A win on all fronts. Though she was willing to live with the worst outcome by being true to herself, the experience ended in the best possible way.

In my opinion, the biggest benefit was in her accepting herself and letting the world see the extraordinary combination of traits, skills and passions that were unique to her. With tears now in my eyes, I thanked her for sharing her story and said I looked forward to following her journey, I had no doubt it was destined to be a big and beautiful one.

You are not one in a million; the truth is you are one in 400 trillion. In a blog post, Dr Ali Binazir took the time to illustrate just how remarkable that is, by explaining the probability of our individual existence: "Imagine there was one life preserver thrown somewhere in some ocean, with exactly one turtle in all of these oceans, swimming underwater somewhere. The probability that you came about is the same as that turtle sticking its head out of the water – into the middle of that life preserver. On one try."

The long and short of it is you are way too special to be a stereotype, so don't act like one.

Creatively Package Your Ideas

Ideas have no material body, but they do have consciousness, and they most certainly have will.

Elizabeth Gilbert, *Big Magic*

I am sure I looked several shades paler, as I responded with the white lie of "absolutely". I was in a meeting with my first ever personal brand coaching client and had just been asked, "Do you have a specific process we will follow?"

I did have an unconscious process, but I hadn't put in the time, effort or thought to write it out and package it up. This is a common issue many of my clients have. When I question what their process or thought leadership is they reply, "I just do what I do, it comes naturally to me."

Now imagine if, going back to the story about my first client, I had responded with, "Yes, I have created a four-step process I call B.O.S.S. and together we will work through each phase." Not only have I valued my ideas and process enough to package them up. It also makes it easy for my client to understand and get on board.

When you creatively package your ideas, it shows that you care about what you are talking about, and you care enough about the person or audience you're dealing with to make sure your approach is clear and easy to understand.

In *Big Magic*, Elizabeth Gilbert proposes that, *"Ideas are a disembodied, energetic life-form."* She goes on to explain, *"Ideas are driven by a single impulse:* to be made manifest. And the only way an idea can be made manifest in our world is through collaboration with a human partner." I love everything about this notion.

Having an idea is one thing, communicating it is another. Given that ideas need us to bring them to life, taking the time to properly package your idea is so important. Here are a few ideas and examples to consider.

Create your own acronym

Brene Brown is famous for this and, yes, it was what inspired me to create the **B.O.S.S.** framework. It stands for **B**e your future self, **O**wn your story, **S**erve an audience and **S**eek a platform. I have presented this exact formula to teams from many multi-national brands. It's so easy and effective and, if you happen to be presenting, it is also a great way for you to remember what you're talking about!

Harness the power of alliteration

Daniel Priestley, author of *Key Person of Influence*, refers to a Key Person of Influence as being an industry KPI, a human benchmark for others to look up to (clever play on another acronym!). He also created a 5-step method he refers to as: **P**itch, **P**ublish, **P**roduct, **P**rofile and **P**artnership. I will add a **P** to that: **P**erfect!

Break it down into numbered steps

Anyone in the personal and professional development space will have read and know about the *7 Habits of Highly Effective People*. If its author, Stephen Covey, had used the title 'Habits of Highly Effective People', I don't think it would have been such a phenomenon. Just knowing there is a start and a finish makes something more achievable. I should also add that numbered lists make it easier to remember information.

Turn your idea into a method and way of life

Tidying up was something I previously disliked, so I must hand it to Marie Kondo – the way she packaged up that idea made me look forward to the process! Rather than just talking about the benefits of cleaning up, she created the KonMari Method which inspired a global movement, a series of internationally bestselling books, and a thriving business.

You have ideas and they have partnered with you for a reason. You are the perfect person to bring them to life and, when you take the time to package them up, you let the people around you know that they are valuable and worth listening to, because they are. *You* are.

What ideas are waiting for you to bring them to life?

Put a Higher Value on Things You Find Easy

> *If I do a job in 30 minutes, it's because it took me*
> *10 years to learn how to do it in 30 minutes.*
> *You owe me for the years, not the minutes.*
>
> **Anonymous**

A dear friend and colleague started her own PR consultancy and was working on the launch of an international jewellery brand. Unfortunately, the client was slow to pay and not appreciative of her work.

Despite the client not holding up their end of the bargain, my friend continued her efforts because it was 'easy' for her to do so. She had worked for the previous 15 years on developing incredible relationships with Australia's top tier media. For her to set up a meeting with *Vogue*, *Australian Financial Review* or *Marie Claire* was 'easy', but only because she had spent years building the relationships.

Her client was not only paying for her time but also for her experience and the value she brought to the project. The problem was, she herself didn't recognise how much that value was worth.

What you find easy is only easy because you have spent years refining your skills. What you consider 'general' knowledge only seems that way because you have been living and breathing this know-how for most of your career. In the world of psychology, this is referred to as the 'The Common Knowledge Trap': we think that what we know is common knowledge and so don't appreciate it in ourselves as much as we should or think of it as something that others might value.

When it comes to living a bigger life, this is a very important point to understand: **we can't live big when we think small**.

I suggested my friend put her pen down and stop all work until her client upheld their end of the bargain. Just as I expected, things quickly changed; they began to value her, because she began to put more value on herself. This approach has nothing to do with being difficult; it has everything to do with knowing your worth and standing by your value. In the words of motivational speaker, Mel Robbins, *"There will always be someone who can't see your worth. Don't let it be you."*

> *What you consider general knowledge, only seems that way because you have been living and breathing this know-how for most of your career.*

In the area of business and career, your sense of self-worth, or lack of it, is also reflected in how much you charge. Without knowing it, the dollar value you place on your time will have a dramatic impact on your perceived value. Which means that sometimes in your bid to be virtuous and fair, you inadvertently send the wrong message to the world.

Think about it like this. Imagine you have booked 2 separate sessions with 2 separate coaches. One is $100 per hour, the other is $1000/hr. Which will you be expecting to get more from? Both might say the same thing, but your expectations and the way you prime yourself in the lead up to the session will impact the outcome. You will be more likely to listen carefully and take notes in the session you have invested more in.

In *The Prosperous Coach*, author Rich Litvin says, "Free advice is usually taken with a grain of salt. But a paid session can change someone's life forever." I agree with this statement. When someone is investing to hear, learn and work with you, they place more value on it.

Think about the things you find easy and effortless, then consider how many years it has taken for you to build your body of knowledge and skills. If you must, break it down into hours spent. Perhaps then you will have a more realistic perspective on what it really took for you to get to the point of 'easy'.

Become Selectively Famous

I am more interested in being good than being famous.

Anne Leibovitz, *portrait photographer*

I know what it is like to be famous. To be clear, I wasn't the famous one, my clients were.

With some clients, one minute we would be in a room filled with their fans, unable to walk an inch without being asked for a photo or signature. Soon after, we'd be in a restaurant both enjoying complete anonymity. On the other hand, I had clients who needed security to walk down the street. I know who I would prefer to be.

In 2008, founding executive editor of *Wired Magazine*, Kevin Kelly, published an essay on his popular blog titled *1000 True Fans*. Ironically, it went viral. The premise of the essay is summed up in his opening paragraph: "To be a successful creator you don't need millions. You don't need millions of dollars or millions of customers, millions of clients, or millions of fans. To make a living as a craftsperson, photographer, musician, designer, author, animator, app maker, entrepreneur, or inventor you need only thousands of true fans." Though social media has made it possible to reach almost any individual everywhere, the reality is we don't need to reach everyone.

In a world where vanity metrics have become a form of social currency and followers have become a measurement of success, intelligent individuals are being led to underestimate the value of their personal brand on social media. They assume a handful of followers suggests failure. Yet, according to Kelly, if that proverbial handful is made up of true fans, then they are on a winning path.

This is at the heart of what it means to be **selectively famous**. It is about making sure you are connecting with the people and audiences that matter. The goal is not strictly about being well known, it is about making the right people aware that you are worth knowing. Keep in mind, the only way to create a true fan is to add value and create a mutually beneficial direct connection.

So where does one start on the road to becoming selectively famous?

Tell 10 of the right people what you are up to

Seth Godin, international bestselling author of *Purple Cow* and *The Dip*, famously talks about "the first 10". This simple marketing theory involves telling 10 people who already know, trust and like you what you are doing. In his words, "If they don't tell anybody else, it's not that good and you should start over. If they do tell other people, you're on your way."

This is about harnessing the power of word of mouth and what is referred to in psychology as the 'halo effect'. If your first 10 people who know, like and trust you, each tell 10 people who know, like and trust them, you are already well on your way to 100 true fans.

Create a spreadsheet

Though spreadsheets don't generally inspire joy, this is where we get organised for a worthwhile cause. Make a list of everyone you want to connect with and go forth to make it happen. If you are questioning whether this is worthwhile, let me introduce you to Stuart Cook.

A serial entrepreneur and former CEO of Zambrero, Cook created a list of all the CEOs he wanted to meet and learn from. He reached out to 70-80 different CEOs that he admired, and they all agreed to meet with him. When asked for any advice he would give to those looking to do the same thing, Cook said, "Go prepared, be likeable and be memorable." Each meeting, whether over the phone or in person, was followed up by a handwritten note of thanks, and Cook remains in touch.

Join an association or network and focus on making the most of that audience

It is impossible to be everywhere all the time and talking to everyone. This is about finding your tribe and going deep rather than wide. Research the relevant associations, groups and networks you feel resonate with who you are and what you do. Then make a concerted effort to attend all their events and get involved. This step is backed by science, as it is all about taking advantage of the familiarity principle and the mere exposure effect. In summary, people like those they are familiar with and the more familiar they are, the more they like them!

On your way to becoming selectively famous, or even famous if that is what you dream of, remember to enjoy the freedom of anonymity in the beginning. This is a lesson that really hit home for me while living in New York City.

> *On your way to becoming selectively famous, or even famous if that is what you dream of, remember to enjoy the freedom of anonymity in the beginning.*

As anyone who has travelled or lived in NYC will confirm, you never know who you are going to meet while you are there. I decided I wanted to live there after watching a guy walk down the street in SoHo wearing only underwear and a traditional American Indian headpiece. No one turned their head or paid any attention. It was just another day in the city that never sleeps (or gets dressed).

I was captivated by the idea of feeling so free, and excited by who I would give myself permission to be when I knew no one was watching. I never officially met the half-dressed man, but I made lots of other new and exciting friends while I was there.

My lesson in appreciating anonymity came through a friend who had just been through a very public divorce with an A-list celebrity. While out together one day, we had an unfortunate run-in with a paparazzi photographer. Far from being a great photo opportunity, my friend felt harassed and frustrated. They confided that they didn't realise how much they loved anonymity until they lost it. That really stuck with me.

At this point you might be confused and wondering how on one hand I am encouraging the idea of becoming known, and on the other celebrating anonymity. My intention in telling the story is not for you to forever remain anonymous. Instead, become intentional about who you want to be known to, and don't assume that the bigger the number, the better. It all comes back to your personal goals and objectives.

Enjoy the freedom of not being known on the path to becoming known. Experiment more, try new things, and don't get caught up worrying who is thinking what about you. As they say, you will be judged regardless, so you might as well be judged for doing something you want to do. Focus on reaching your 1000 true fans and start living the benefits of being selectively famous.

Lead Thought in the Way Only You Can

Leadership is not about titles, positions, or flowcharts. It is about one life influencing another.

John C Maxwell, author and orator

I don't like the term 'thought leader'. It can feel like another title or position we should be aspiring to achieve. Sadly, many people disqualify themselves from even trying to become a thought leader, because they don't think they can live up to what being a thought leader entails.

I prefer to switch it around and use the term 'leading thought'. In my opinion, this better describes the aim of the game. Rather than see it as another title or position to achieve, we turn it into action and level out the playing field.

The simple act of sharing your opinions, ideas and expertise is an act of leading the thoughts of others. The questions are: Are you doing so for a purpose? Do you have a bigger vision for the ideas you are sharing? And how do you want to impact the person or people you are sharing your ideas with?

By shifting the focus and appreciating the privilege of gaining influence and leading the thoughts of others, your priority here is being of service. Any accolades or recognition achieved become secondary.

I find it hard to believe that iconic individuals, such as Oprah, Nelson Mandela, Martin Luther King and Barack Obama, were driven by the single goal of becoming a thought leader. Instead, their sole focus was leading the thoughts of others in a way that would enhance the lives of their audience. The more people bought into their ideas, the more influence and recognition they achieved. In the wise words of Simon Sinek, bestselling author of *Start with Why*: *A boss has a title; a leader has the people.*

There was a time in history where leading the thoughts of others was a privilege reserved for the few. Today, in most parts of the Western world, we are not only given the freedom of speech, but we also have access to platforms that allow us to reach individuals all over the world. With that, we have been given the opportunity to lead the thoughts of others anytime we like.

On the path to doing so there are several **unhelpful myths** I suggest you let go of:

- **You have to be a leader in your field to lead thought.** Experience is a wonderful thing to have, but it can also be a hindrance. Lack of experience gives you the ability to see something with fresh eyes. I recently spoke to students at a leading university and could not stress enough the importance of their embracing the power of their youth. I reminded them that their lack of experience may be the reason they come up with new ideas!

- **You have to be an extrovert to lead thought.** In the business world, some of the most successful founders, leaders and industry advocates are introverts, including the likes of Bill Gates and Warren Buffett. If that is not convincing enough, according to an article in *Inc.* magazine here are some other well-known introverts who put themselves out there: Meryl Streep, Steven Spielberg, Oprah, Al Gore, Elon Musk, Steve Wozniak and Marissa Mayer. Case closed.

- **You have to have all the answers to lead thought.** Sharing your ideas is not about knowing it all. It is about contributing to the collective conversation for the betterment of everyone. In the words of Eleanor Roosevelt, "Great minds discuss ideas; average minds discuss events; small minds discuss people." There is no one in this universe who has precisely the same life and career experiences as you, therefore your perspective and story have value.

You have a voice, you have a platform, so why not give back and do your part in leading the thoughts of others in a way that will enhance their life? You benefit from the exposure and expanding network, and the audience benefits from what you have to share. Who knows? You might even become a thought leader.

Be Consistent with What You Share Online

Success doesn't come from what you do occasionally. It comes from what you do consistently.

Marie Forleo, *entrepreneur and philanthropist*

My grandmother loved Danielle Steel novels. I vividly remember that, as children, my brother and I would go through them and laugh uncontrollably at the saucy bits. I would not be able to tell you how many books she had, but let's just say I am pretty sure she was Danielle Steel's biggest fan.

Despite my grandmother's love of Danielle Steel's talent for writing and everything else she knew about her as an author, I doubt she would continue to follow Danielle Steel if she suddenly decided to write science fiction. You may already be guessing where I'm going with this.

When it comes to developing a personal brand on social media, your content speaks volumes. What you post about once or twice is often inconsequential; it is what you consistently post about that begins to shape what others expect from you. If you are confused about the direction, message or overall purpose of your content, chances are anyone who follows you will feel just as confused.

My recommendation is that you work with the magic number 3. That is, you decide on up to 3 pillars of content to focus on with your social media presence. For example, my 3 pillars are personal branding, influence and communication. I rarely post about parenting, my family, my health or my wellness routine. If I do, I will always link it back to one of my pillars. Though you may change those 3 pillars over time, it is important to create consistent and cohesive messaging.

If you are worried you don't have anything new to say, don't be. Just remember the fact that you are saying what you are saying in your own voice, through the lens of your own personal experience, makes it new.

If you are worried the content won't be good enough, chances are in the beginning it won't be. Like any skill, creating content and finding your unique way of communicating takes time. Be willing to experiment and don't try to reinvent the wheel. Look at what others are doing and work on ways to make their framework and approach your own.

As someone who was adamant social media was never going to be 'my thing', I am happy I changed my mind. Through social media platforms, I have been able to connect with inspiring, like-hearted individuals and some of my favourite clients. Opportunities I never knew existed have emerged because I consistently show up and share.

It took time, lots of cringe, truckloads of fear, and a ridiculous amount of overthinking to get to the point where sharing on social media has become second nature. For anyone over 40, there is no avoiding the uncomfortable fact that we are not social media natives. You might want to believe it is just not you, so that is a decision you keep buying into. Ask yourself whether this viewpoint is serving you?

I decided to look further into Danielle Steel and discovered she has published 179 books since 1973 and sold 650 million copies worldwide! Interestingly, she has this sign hanging up in her office: *There are no miracles. There is only discipline.* Being consistent takes discipline and I promise you it pays off.

> *There are no miracles.*
> *There is only discipline.*

Creating a personal brand takes time and intentional effort. You are building an asset you can take with you wherever you go, and consistency is what will create results. Be the person you want to follow on social media and you will be amazed by what can happen, even when you sleep!

I have had potential new clients reach out from all over the world because of something I posted online (even months after the fact). James Clear, author of *Atomic Habits* put it perfectly in a podcast interview with Tim Ferris, when he referred to social media content as "work that keeps working for you". He explained, "It's almost like there are multiple versions of James out there and they're all continuing to work right now. That's an example of the work that keeps working for you."

In the beginning, the effort needed to put yourself out there may outweigh the results. But just remember, you are building a portfolio and giving your online self everything it needs to make your dreams come true, even when you are literally in bed dreaming.

Download my free Brand Identity Guide worksheet by visiting – http://www.carliilyon.com/brandidentityguide

Learn to Network from the Stage

Public speaking is an asset that will last you 50 or 60 years.

Warren Buffett, *businessman and philanthropist*

I clearly remember the first time I got up to speak. My voice trembling, hands shaking, and little waterfalls of sweat dripping from under my arms to my waist. A friend of mine invited me to present to all the women in their family business for International Women's Day and I didn't want to let her down. I had no choice but to continue.

I threw myself into the presentation and eventually found my flow. I looked out at the 50 or so women in the room and decided to put all my focus, and channel all my energy, towards them. By the end, I couldn't wait to do it all over again.

I have always considered myself introverted, which is why I never in a million years thought I would end up as a speaker. Yet when I am on stage, I feel like a completely different person. The fact I am up there in my own space and in control of the narrative makes it work for me.

Networking and putting yourself out there are part of living a big life, and speaking is a wonderful way to become more visible. Rather than working a room at a crowded event, you can let the whole room know who you are, what you stand for, and what you have to offer.

My first speaking opportunity taught me that you should never judge who you think you will be in a certain situation, environment and/or role, until you have experienced that situation. In his incredible book *The End of Average*, Todd Rose, who previously led the Laboratory for the Science of Individuality at Harvard, explores the "context principle". In the book, he explains: "behavior is not determined by traits or the situation but emerges out of the unique interaction between the two."

This means you can't know precisely how you will be in any given context, situation or experience until you put yourself out (or in) there to try it. It doesn't mean you won't have your moments of challenge; trust me, I have had plenty of those. One comes to mind and even that ended up being a blessing.

> *You can't know precisely how you will be in any given context, situation or experience until you put yourself out (or in) there to try it.*

They looked at me and waited. As a speaker, it is the moment you dread most. I stood there, mind blank, and quickly excused myself. I had just been about to start a personal branding workshop, and nerves got the better of me.

Once outside the room, I honestly considered running away, even though on the other side of the door there was a room full of people who had paid to listen to me speak. Knowing that running away was not an option, I took a deep breath, walked back in, smiled, and started again (or at least for the first time). Fear faced, still alive, the workshop ended up being a great success.

It would be easy for me talk about the importance of facing your fears, but that would be too obvious. The biggest lesson I learned that day would come after the workshop ended. One of the participants admitted to me they could see I was struggling at the beginning. They went on to say they felt my pain and wanted to follow me outside, but knew I just had to go through it. I realised in that moment, by falling to pieces and pulling myself back together again, I'd demonstrated to everyone in the room that life is about progress, not perfection. The mistake was personal, the lesson was a benefit for us all.

> *By falling to pieces and pulling myself back together again, I'd demonstrated to everyone that life is about progress, not perfection.*

For many people, fear of public speaking has come from a negative experience they had in the past. Let me give you an example from a client of mine I will call Natalie.

"I hate speaking in public, so I always present sitting down," Natalie admitted to me in a coaching session.

I carefully explained the chances of Natalie commanding a room - and being perceived as a leader - were minimal while seated. I then asked her to explain the last time she tried speaking while standing up. I was shocked when she admitted it had been more than 5 years earlier!

After agreeing she was not the same person she was 5 years ago, Natalie committed to challenging her outdated assumptions. As you have probably guessed, the next time she spoke, she stood up and thoroughly enjoyed speaking. The experience and self-induced challenge allowed Natalie to show up as the leader she was aspiring to be and prove to herself she could do it.

As we grow, evolve and change, it is important to recognise who we were yesterday is not who we are today; who we want to be in the future, should not be limited by who we were in the past. One bad experience in the past should not stop you from pursuing new and worthwhile experiences today or tomorrow. If you have had a bad experience public speaking in the past, be sure to challenge yourself to try again.

> *As we grow, evolve and change, it is important to recognise who we were yesterday is not who we are today.*

If you are willing to try this strategy for yourself and network from the stage, I suggest you consider the following 4 steps (you will also find recommended reading at the end of this book):

Step 1: Make it known that you are a 'speaker'

Whether it is in your social media headline, summary or content. Making it known that you are available to speak is a very important first step. Do I recommend you do this even before you have delivered one talk? Yes (this is all presuming you have something you want to say!). Think of it as a 'build it and they will come' scenario.

Step 2: Package what you have to say into 1 to 3 different talks

Make it easy for the people you know, and are reaching out to, by clearly outlining what you have to say, the key takeaways, and the ultimate outcomes of your talk/s. Reach out to your network via email.

Step 3: Consistently create relevant content on social media

One of the best ways to promote your talk is to turn it into bite-size pieces of social media content that offer a preview of what you speak about. You can do this by making sure you capture video footage and images of you speaking.

Step 4: Get listed with relevant speakers' bureaus

A colleague of mine who runs a very successful speakers' bureau suggested that, before you can be considered as a speaker with the bureau, you need to have delivered a minimum 20-50 talks. You will also need to up your marketing game by creating a professional speaker reel, speaker bio, and have relevant testimonials to share.

You will never really know whether this strategy will work for you until you give it a go. I hope this has inspired you to do so. What topic would you like to share from the stage?

Master the Art of Asking for What You Want

You get in life what you have the courage to ask for.

Oprah Winfrey, *talk show host and producer*

My husband, Dom, is a master at asking for what he wants. He has no shame in asking and has always had the philosophy: *If you don't ask, you don't get.* It has led him (and us) to enjoy countless upgrades, be offered money-can't-buy experiences, and receive massive discounts. It is one of the qualities I love most about him and, to be honest, I am still learning to master it.

When it comes to building a personal brand and putting yourself out there, my experience as a former international publicist taught me that you can't wait for opportunities to come to you; success comes from asking, pitching and seeking the opportunities you want. My high-profile clients had no hesitation in paying me handsomely to ask, pitch and seek opportunities on their behalf.

I understood that asking for what you want and chasing opportunities was the unquestionable path to success, yet for most of my career I did the opposite. I insisted on waiting.

Waiting for permission. Waiting for validation. Waiting for opportunities to land in my lap.

I have many clients who are guilty of doing the same thing. This reminds me of a client I will call Lydia. Lydia was an extremely talented speaker and a rising star. We were overhauling her LinkedIn and updating all her personal branding communication assets. We were also starting to strategically think about the things we wanted and needed to do to position her correctly.

As the conversation progressed, I heard a pattern emerging. See if you can spot it.

Me: *Have you pitched to speak at TEDx?*

Lydia: *No, I assumed they would ask me.*

Me: *Have you ever reached out to Forbes or anyone you know who has a link to the publication?*

Lydia: *No, I assumed they would approach me to contribute.*

Me: *Have you asked that colleague for a testimonial or character reference?*

Lydia: *No, I assumed they would offer me one, if they felt they wanted to.*

Lydia made the mistake of thinking opportunities would come to her and that her good work would speak for itself.

If you have an idea, pitch it. If you want something, ask for it. If you need help, let others know. Never assume anything and don't expect others to know what you need, want or are looking for.

Here is a short list of examples where 'asking' is relevant to personal branding:

- Asking a client for a testimonial
- Asking a colleague to make a recommendation
- Asking a friend to offer you a favour or introduction to someone
- Asking a business associate for an opportunity

The list goes on and on.

Unless you ask, it is very unlikely any of the above will happen. The people around you, aside from a precious few, don't know what you are up to and, importantly, what you need. If you don't ask, they are going to assume you don't need or want their help.

If asking for help is a weakness of yours, it would be worth noting that research has shown that asking someone for a favour can end up with them liking you more! It is called the Ben Franklin effect. It seems that making others feel wanted, needed and helpful is a win-win outcome for everyone involved.

> *Success comes in asking, pitching and seeking the opportunities you want.*

There is asking and then there is pitching. Not so much like comparing apples and oranges, more like different versions of apples. I dare say, a pitch is typically more formal and crafted in a specific way.

When it comes to personal branding and putting yourself out there, just like asking, pitching is par for the course. Whether it is pitching to speak, feature on a podcast, instigate media coverage, or secure any form of professional opportunity, putting together a well thought out pitch can mean the difference between getting what you want and forever wondering 'what if'. You also never know what new doors and connections will emerge.

I met my best friend Jesse as the result of a cold call and well-crafted pitch. I was representing Australia's first ever at-home diabetes test, and she was the National PR Manager of Fitness First at the time. I was pitching a brand partnership, and we often joke about how scary she was over the phone. I persisted in following up and the partnership became a national success, both personally and professionally. Jesse ended up being my maid of honour when I married, to put the closeness of our friendship into perspective.

I always think back to that experience whenever I am pitching for new opportunities but not because I am under the illusion that every person I pitch to will become my best friend! I think back to it because I want to remain open to the unexpected benefits, as opposed to the fear and discomfort, of pitching itself.

So how do you craft the perfect pitch and create new opportunities? Here are my top 3 tips:

1. Do your research first.

Take the time to really understand the company and/or individual you are pitching to. This is where social media is helpful. You can gain valuable insight into what they are doing, who they are doing it with, and where you might be able to fit in. You can use those details in the pitch to show the effort you have made.

2. Make sure your pitch is short, sharp and to the point.

There is nothing worse than a long-winded pitch. Aim for 2-3 short paragraphs max and make sure your first sentence clearly sums up your idea. The second needs to introduce who you are and establish credibility (name dropping, mentioning previous clients and any other important achievements might help here). You then need to explain why you are the perfect person to partner and/or work with and potential next steps.

3. If in writing, pitch via email (not social platforms) and always follow up.

You can find just about anyone's email address by searching online. Always pitch via email and make sure you follow up. How soon after you follow up really depends on how time-sensitive the pitch is. I usually wait a week to follow up the first time and am not afraid to follow up several times after that. People are often busy and drowning in emails; timing is everything, which is why following up is so effective.

Success and getting what you want are never guaranteed, but you can be sure you won't get what you want if you never ask, pitch or seek the opportunities you want.

As the saying goes …

The universe has only 3 answers when you ask for what you want:

Yes

No

I have something better in mind

So, what are you going to ask for this week?

You can access my free Power Pitch framework by visiting **www.carliilyon.com/powerpitchframework**

Invite a New Network into Your Life

In a world of algorithms, hashtags and followers, know the true importance of human connection.

Simi Fromen, *writer and wellness coach*

I wish I could tell you it happened gradually. But that was not the case at all. It happened instantly and conspicuously, leaving me stunned and insecure. I knew I would face change; I just didn't realise how personal it would feel.

Being a mum was always one of my biggest goals. After having our first son, Francesco, I was confident I could find a way to balance work and parenting. When we fell pregnant with number 2, I wasn't feeling as confident. My work required me to be available at all hours and I knew something had to give.

I was blessed with options and decided it was time to take extended maternity leave. I gave all my clients ample notice and by the time Alessandro came into the world, I was officially a full-time mother of two beautiful boys under 2.

That was when the phone stopped ringing, and the invites stopped coming. Of course, I was prepared for that. What I wasn't prepared for was that my calls would go unanswered, and my emails left with no response. Individuals I had counted as friends seemed to disappear without a trace.

Not only was I left questioning my worth and identity, but I was also confronted with the harsh reality that many of the characters in my working life had been there conditionally. Now that I couldn't help them get what they wanted, I was of no value to them.

My father once told me about a colleague of his who was a senior executive at one of Australia's leading retail brands. He was made redundant after the company was acquired and found himself without a role. Dad made a point of staying in touch, even though there was no immediate incentive. Just under a year later, the aforementioned colleague was appointed as CEO of another iconic brand. He called my dad to say thank you and went on to explain, "I didn't hear from anyone after I was made redundant; you were one of the few people who stayed in touch."

In telling me this story, my father was teaching me a lesson about integrity and the importance of valuing the people in your life – not just for their role title and status, but for their humanity. My personal experience cemented this lesson even more deeply.

Rather than becoming bitter, I found reasons to be grateful. Life had offered me a cosmic filter, allowing more time and space to connect with the people who mattered.

> *Rather than become bitter,
> I found reasons to be grateful.*

After our boys were happily settled at pre-school, it was time for me to get back into the world of work. I had to rebuild my professional identity and broaden my network. I couldn't wait for the invites to come to me (I had given up on them a long time ago); it was time for me to invite a new network into my life. Perhaps it is time for you to do the same?

In his book *You're Invited*, behavioural scientist Jon Levy writes: The most universal strategy for success is creating meaningful connections with those who can impact you, your life, and the things you care about.

Levy is the founder of The Influencers Dinner, one of the most exclusive dining experiences in the world. Hosted in 11 locations across 4 countries and with over 225 dinners held, Levy recognised the importance of inviting the right network into your life and has created a platform to help others do the same.

Twelve strangers are invited to cook a meal together on the condition they can't talk about their career or give their last names. What started as a small group quickly turned into a movement and the hottest invite in town. Levy shaped a network of industry experts, Nobel laureates, celebrities, Olympic medallists, musicians, artists and even the occasional member of the royal family – all with the mission of having a positive impact on each other and the world.

What I love most about this story is that it all started in Levy's own home in New York City.

When it comes to personal branding and living a bigger life, proactively shaping your network is vital. I am also here to tell you that it doesn't have to feel self-serving and superficial. Some of my best opportunities have come from the most unexpected places and connections.

Author and keynote speaker, Dorie Clark, summed it up perfectly in her book *The Long Game*, where she recommends *'infinite horizon networking'*. In her words: It's pure, no-agenda relationship building. Because when you have zero goals or expectations – only a fundamental interest in who the person is – you can enjoy the experience and let it unfold organically. All that matters is that the person is like-hearted, and your values are aligned.

Dom is a natural at this without even knowing it. His network is rich with like-hearted individuals from all walks of life. From farmers to property developers, entrepreneurs to entertainers, and celebrities to construction workers. Dom doesn't connect with a person based on what they do, it all comes down to who they are. If there is something you want done in any area of life, chances are Dom has a contact who can help make it happen.

Most people make the mistake of limiting their network to the industry they are in, which means the opportunities they attract and the information they have access to are also limited. When I was in the world of PR, my world felt small. I honestly thought I knew everyone, at least in Australia. One of the best parts of the business I have today is connecting with, and learning from, individuals from different industries worldwide. My network is expanding in a vast array of directions, and I am being intentional about that.

If you find yourself limited by your network, only you have the power to make a change. It starts with inviting a new network into your life. Whether it is reaching out to one person and asking them to have a coffee or hosting an event and bringing a group of new people together. On one hand, you need to get better at sending invites; on the other, it is important to say 'yes' to invites you receive.

A colleague of mine said it perfectly when she confided, "I always feel better after I attend a networking event. I walk away feeling inspired. The problem is saying 'yes' to the invite and making myself go."

As an introvert, I get it. It can feel overwhelming to put yourself out there and attend events, especially when you don't know anyone else in the room. In those instances, I find it helpful to remind myself that most people feel the same way. By focusing on others, it takes the spotlight off any insecurities you have and firmly places it on making the other person feel good about themselves. By doing so, you will naturally ask more questions, listen attentively, and enjoy the process of learning something new about someone new.

I came across this quote: *When you least expect it, you could meet someone who will completely change your life.*

How true that is. You still haven't met all the people destined to impact your life in ways you can't imagine.

The life you want and the dreams you wish to manifest may rest in the hands of individuals you are yet to encounter. With each invitation extended and accepted, be open to all that life has to offer in the form of a new connection. And importantly, be generous in giving all you can to those you meet along the way.

Celebrate Rejection and Criticism

*There is only one way to avoid criticism:
do nothing, say nothing, and be nothing.*

Aristotle, Ancient Greek philosopher

I spent most of my career seeking approval and avoiding criticism. As unrealistic as it sounds, having everyone's approval was of paramount importance, even when it meant going against my own better judgement. It wasn't just my family, friends and colleagues I worried about; it was sometimes people I admired from afar. I know I am not alone and have had many clients admit they do the same.

The irony is, when you start reading, researching and meeting successful individuals, you quickly discover that criticism and rejection are a rite of passage to success. At some point, these successful individuals had to tune into what they felt was right and tune out all the naysayers who disagreed.

At some point, these successful individuals had to tune into what they felt was right and tune out all the naysayers that disagreed.

This reminds me of a story a friend shared with me. My friend is considered a fitness business guru and would be the perfect mentor if you were planning to enter that space. Several years ago, a colleague of theirs came to them with a business idea. My friend rejected the idea and, in their own words, advised their colleague that "it would not work". Their colleague decided to go ahead regardless of the negative feedback and ended up building a global fitness community with 2,000 studios in 66 countries.

The buzzword right now, especially in business, is 'disruption'. By its very definition, it is a 'disturbance or problem that interrupts an event, activity or process'. Change and new ideas will inevitably receive the disapproval and rejection of those happy to maintain things just as they are. This includes the 'experts' we often listen to above our own intuition and experience.

Making decisions in the face of disapproval and rejection is never easy. It is something we are confronted with in business and life all the time. While it is wonderful to gain recognition, approval and acceptance from those around you, when you give yourself all these things first and foremost, you are in a real position of personal empowerment. This was a lesson a client of mine had to learn the hard way. I will call her Tina.

Tina had been diligently working on her personal brand. She made the decision to start putting herself out there as a speaker to share her remarkable personal story. Her website was completed, social media platforms updated, and launch letter ready to go, when her best friend dropped a bombshell.

Her best friend said she thought Tina was crazy. She suggested Tina put everything on hold. She even went as far as saying that Tina's decision to put herself out there and create a personal brand would ruin her existing financial planning business. In other words, Tina's best friend was expressing her disapproval.

It was not the first time I had seen or heard this. I often suggest clients be prepared; when they start building their profile, it will potentially be their closest friends and family who will criticise and disapprove first!

Tina followed her intuition, launched her brand, wrote a bestselling book, and today is regularly invited to speak. A whole new and exciting world emerged because she ignored the criticism and put faith in her own decision.

No matter what you do, how you do it, why you do it or when you do it, if you play big enough, you will inevitably receive rejection and criticism. It is a sign you are growing and playing big. That is something to celebrate.

> *If you play big enough, you will inevitably receive rejection and criticism. It is a sign you are growing and playing big. That is something to celebrate.*

My former client, Dr John Demartini, says: *No matter what you say or do, you will always have a balance of support and challenge. The bigger the game you play, the more challenge you will face.*

Imagine if we were to look upon certain forms of disapproval and rejection in our lives symbolically, rather than taking it personally. What if we even expected disapproval and rejection as progress and began to see it as a good thing – a sign that our influence is growing, in line with the level of disapproval and rejection that surrounds us.

Here are 3 ideas that will help you reframe criticism and rejection:

- **It is a sign you have created something new.**

    Know this for a fact – automobiles, bicycles, umbrellas, planes and even the trusty lightbulb (and the people behind them) all faced suspicion, criticism and outright rejection at some stage. Things we today consider everyday 'can't live without' items were once too 'new' to be embraced by everyone.

- **It is a sign your sphere of influence has expanded.**

    Look at the individuals who have made their mark on the world to know this to be true. Take anyone you admire in the public arena and research the criticism and rejection they have received. Even Mother Teresa had her critics!

- **It is a sign your goals are big and ambitious.**

    Your big thinking and ambitious action may upset those around you. You have a decision to make; is it them or your future self you need to pay attention to? Choose your future self, and I promise you your future self will thank you for it.

Remember, the people who remain in your life to witness and support your growth are the ones who matter most.

All signs lead to knowing and believing that disapproval, rejection and criticism are not something we should avoid. Instead, they are to be celebrated for all the reasons mentioned above. You are not here to serve and please everyone. Focus first on being true to yourself and know, in doing so, you will attract the people and opportunities that are truly right.

No matter what you do, how you do it, why you do it or when you do it, if you play big enough, you will inevitably receive rejection and criticism. It is a sign you are growing and playing big, and that is something to celebrate.

Never Put a Deadline on Becoming the Best Version of Yourself

It is never too late to reinvent yourself. Start a new career at 40. Fall in love at 50. Learn to dance at 60. Start a whole new life at 70. Stop saying you can't. You can and you should. Dreams don't have an expiration date.

Ravenwolf, *writer and spiritual practitioner*

When I first launched my personal brand and the business I have today, I set myself a deadline of 3 years. That, I thought, was the magical number to determine if I had something the market wanted. I had big goals and aspirations. If I was good enough, I thought, things would happen quickly.

The 3-year timeline was inspired after reading that Simon Sinek had been invited to deliver a TEDx talk after speaking for 3 years (often in friends' lounge rooms). His TEDx talk went on to be viewed 60 million times!

At the time of writing this book, I am 7 years in, and I can see how the crazy deadline I set has often made me feel like a failure. My expectations were so high, and the odds stacked firmly against me.

> *I can see how the crazy deadline I set has
> often made me feel like a failure.*

On the days I especially feel like giving up, I always think of my favourite author, Steven Pressfield, who I have mentioned in this book already. Pressfield had been writing unsuccessfully for decades before he published his first novel at 52. The book became a big hit and was made into a movie, directed by Robert Redford and starring Will Smith and Matt Damon.

It took Steven 28 hard years to experience an 'overnight success' and go on to sell millions of books. Prior to reaching commercial success as a writer, he drove a tractor, he was a teacher, a copywriter and picked fruit as a migrant worker. He never gave up on his dreams and used his setbacks to make him better, not bitter.

They say a goal without a deadline is simply a wish, yet I would warn against putting a deadline on some of your dreams. This is especially relevant when it comes to personal branding and putting yourself out there. Everything takes time, and it will likely take longer than you think for there to be a tipping point resembling success.

Don't give up. Have the courage to use your setbacks to make you better and let go of unrealistic timelines that constantly make you feel like you are failing. There is no deadline to becoming the best version of yourself, so keep trying.

Conclusion

There is only one of you in all time.

Martha Graham, *dancer and choreographer*

I launched my first ever personal branding workshop on the 8/8/2018. I was hoping numerology would work in my favour, 8 being a lucky number. I wanted it to be a success and on many levels it was. I had 11 women in the room, and it was the beginning of a new career path. I was excited about what the future would hold.

A week later, my best friend passed away unexpectedly.

More than a friend, Judith was family to me. She was there by my side through some of the biggest moments in my life. Judith helped decorate my first ever apartment, wholeheartedly approved of my choice of husband, was the first person I called when I found out I was having a baby, was there to massage my swollen feet when I was pregnant, and is godmother to our first-born son, Francesco.

Judith had been travelling in Italy where she experienced health challenges and was admitted to hospital as soon as she returned home. As far as we were all concerned, it was just precautionary. I spoke to Judith on the Wednesday and on Friday she was gone. I will never forget the moment her husband Mark called to let me know she had passed away; it haunts me to this day.

What also haunts me was knowing Judith was on the precipice of launching a namesake brand. As a pioneer in the world of aromatherapy, Judith was planning to take all her hard-earned experience and bottle it up. Literally.

At her funeral, her eldest son Jacob came up to me and held out a vial of body oil; it was a sample from Judith's skincare range. On it was a small sticker with the words *magnum opus*, translated to mean 'most important or best work'. With Judith gone, the world would now miss out on all of that.

Losing Judith made me confront the reality that time does not wait for anyone. It created a sense of urgency that powers the work I do today, and it has been a big driver in my writing this book. I hope it is an energy that will infuse your actions from this moment on.

It is not about rushing to do everything. It is about making sure you do the things that matter. It is about being who you know you want to be and doing the big things you know you want to do.

At the beginning of this book, I shared with you the opening lines of my favourite children's book *Maybe* by Kobi Yamada. Now let me share the last few lines because they sum up everything I want to say in the most beautifully simple way:

Maybe you have no idea just how good you really can be? And maybe you don't know how much you matter?

But maybe, just maybe, the world has been waiting centuries for someone exactly like you.

One thing is for sure, you are here and because you are here ... anything is possible.

Visibility leads to possibility. Let the world see, hear and know you. There is no time to waste in playing small. You can't serve the world by hiding from it.

In the enduring words of Shakespeare's *Hamlet*: *To be or not to be, that is the question*. After reading this book, I hope in my heart you have the **Courage to Be**.

With love, *Carlii* xxx

Here is a little poem I wrote just for you...

Wandering Star

If fear and overwhelm ever set in
And you struggle to find the courage to begin

Allow your gaze to rise to the sky beyond
Up to a galaxy held by an unbreakable bond

See the opulent clouds, the twinkle of stars
The bright light of Jupiter, the sunburn of Mars

Behind all you can see is a universe of more
So vast, so magnificent, so infinitely galore

A quantum soup of creation you are a part
Here to experience your greatness if only you'll start

The magic and beauty you see up above
Resides within you, deserving your love

Nurture, explore, and have the *Courage to Be*
The shining bright light the world is waiting to see

Acknowledgements

I have wanted to write a book for as long as I can remember. I have diaries dating back to my early 20s with the goal of being an author listed in black and white. Like everything worthwhile in life, writing this book has been a team effort and there are many people I would like to thank.

First and foremost, my lifelong mentor, Leon Nacson. When I reflect on all the ways Leon has shaped my life and career, I am overwhelmed with awe and gratitude. Over two decades ago, I walked into his office as a young twenty-year-old woman looking for direction and purpose, and he wholeheartedly helped me find it. Writing this book with Leon as my guide has felt like a magical full circle moment. Words of thanks do not even begin to adequately express how I feel. Leon, I wouldn't be who I am, and this book wouldn't be what it is, without you.

Maggie Hamilton, you are referred to as publishing royalty for a reason and writing this book with you in my corner has meant everything to me. Thank you for your nurturing energy and expert direction. Margie Tubbs, thank you for taking my words and making them so much better. To James and the team at Spiffing, thank you for turning this dream into a reality with such grace and expertise. Emma Rusher,

Clare Hallifax, Prue Turnell, Jayden Koulizakis and the team at Audible, what a dream team you are! Prue Aja, Janine De La Zilwa, and Sascha Flook, thank you for your masterful abilities in making everything look sensational.

To my clients and all the amazing individuals I have had the privilege of working with across the globe, thank you. A special mention to Melissa Doyle, Miranda Kerr, Dr John Demartini, Nick Leary, Nat Shehata, Gillian Fox and Andrea Francolini. I love what I do as much as I do because of the people I get to connect with. Your stories and presence inspire me endlessly.

To all my beautiful friends on earth and in heaven, especially Kathryn Eisman (thank you for the subtitle!), Jesse James, Isabella Kleut, and Judith White. As they say, there are friends, there is family, and then there are friends that become family. You have been there by my side for all the big moments, and the story of my life would not be as colourful and enchanting without you in it. Thank you from the bottom of my heart.

To my family, by birth and through marriage. Frank, Pina and the Lopresti clan, thank you for bringing culture, animated conversation, and the best food I have ever eaten into my life. Your unwavering support in all areas is appreciated beyond words.

To Mum, Dad, and my brother, Jay Lyon, thank you for being just the way you are in every way. Everything is possible in life when you are surrounded by unconditional love, and that is what I have always felt from each of you. My love for you is equally unconditional.

Lastly, to my husband, Dom, and sons, Francesco and Alessandro. You are my everything. I married a soulmate and then gave birth to 2 more. I am so proud and honoured to journey through this lifetime with you by my side. You inspire me to be better every day and everything I do feels so much more meaningful because I get to share it with you. I not only dedicate this book to you, I dedicate *me* to you forever. Thank you, I love you.

Recommended Reading

Books That Changed the Way I Think

Briefly Perfectly Human – Alua Arthur

The Top 5 Regrets of the Dying – Bronnie Ware

Into the Magic Shop – James Doty

Mind Magic – James Doty

The Power of Your Subconscious Mind – Joseph Murphy

The Untethered Soul – Michael Singer

Code Name God – Mani Bhaumik

Adapt – Andrea Clarke

Books That Changed the Way I Act

The Charisma Myth – Olivia Fox Cabane

Authentic Gravitas – Rebecca Newton

Trillion Dollar Coach – Eric Schmidt, Jonathan Rosenberg, Alan Eagle

Be Your Future Self Now – Benjamin Hardy

The Alter Ego Effect – Todd Herman

Books That Changed the Way I Show Up in the World

The Big Leap – Gay Hendricks

What they Don't Teach you at Harvard Business School – Mark McCormack

Building a StoryBrand – Donald Miller

Tribes – Seth Godin

TED Talks – Chris Anderson

Let's stay in touch

If you enjoyed this book, I think you will love:

My Newsletter

Each week I share a tip, idea, and/ or a story aimed at helping you find the courage to put yourself out there and do so in the most powerful way possible.

Connecting on socials

Find me on LinkedIn at www.linkedin.com/in/carliilyon/ and Instagram @carlii_lyon

My events and masterclass sessions

My keynotes, masterclasses, and workshops are designed with love to help you show up with purpose and have the *courage to be* visible to the people that matter.

Learn more at www.carliilyon.com

Your #couragetobe moment deserves to be celebrated!

What brave thing did you do to put yourself out there?
I want to hear about it.

Share your story using **#couragetobe** and tag me.

Let's build a community where
courage inspires more courage.

About the Author

For over two decades, Carlii Lyon has been helping remarkable individuals across the globe raise their profile and build influence.

As a former international personal publicist, her past clients include a world-leading supermodel, *New York Times* bestselling authors, inventors, musicians, and even a British celebrity foot reader!

Today, Carlii is dedicated to helping everyday individuals, executives and emerging leaders become individuals of influence and impact by proactively shaping their professional identities, communicating their value, and becoming visible to the audiences that matter. Recognised as a thought leader on the topic, Carlii has been invited to speak to the teams of Top 50 ASX Listed companies and iconic brands internationally; including the likes of *Financial Times*, Spotify, Warner Discovery Group, Volvo, GPT, Microsoft and L'Oréal to name a few. She is a regular contributor to *Forbes Australia* on the topic of personal branding and influence, and has been featured in Smart Company, *CEO Magazine, Sky News* and *The Sunday Telegraph*.

www.ingramcontent.com/pod-product-compliance
Lightning Source LLC
Chambersburg PA
CBHW071238070526
44583CB00017B/2241